D1383984

Honeſty
is the beſt Policy ;
Honeſty
and
Induſtry
perform Wonders.

JOHN NEWBERY
AND HIS BOOKS

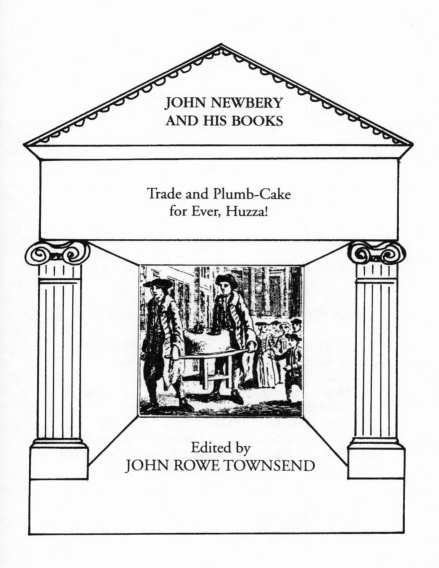

JOHN NEWBERY
AND HIS BOOKS

Trade and Plumb-Cake
for Ever, Huzza!

Edited by
JOHN ROWE TOWNSEND

The Scarecrow Press, Inc.
Metuchen, N.J., & London
1994

British Library Cataloguing-in-Publication Data available

Library of Congress Cataloging-in-Publication Data

John Newbery and his books : trade and plumb-cake for
   ever, huzza! / edited by John Rowe Townsend.
      p.   cm.
   Includes bibliographical references (p.   ) and index.
   ISBN 0-8108-2950-9 (acid-free paper)
   1. Newbery, John, 1713–1767.   2. Children's
literature—Publishing—Great Britain—History—18th
century.   3. Children's literature, English—History and
criticism.   4. Publishers and publishing—Great
Britain—History—18th century.   I. Townsend, John
Rowe.
Z325.N53J64   1994
070.5′0941—dc20   94-23293

First published by Colt Books Ltd 1994
Copyright © 1994 by John Rowe Townsend
Manufactured in the United States of America
Printed on acid-free paper

To
the Little Masters and Misses
whose books were bought from Mr Newbery;

to the "Children Six Foot High"
whom he helped to educate;

and to the sufferers from multifarious ills
who were cured (I hope)
by his medicines

the present work is respectfully
and retrospectively
dedicated

CONTENTS

The churchyard at Waltham St Lawrence and inscription
on John Newbery's tomb

Preface

THERE IS a hint of Dick Whittington, a touch of the Industrious Apprentice, in the story of John Newbery. He was an eighteenth-century farm boy from a small village in Berkshire who went to London and prospered. On the way, he had stopped for a few years at Reading, where he found work with a printer, made himself indispensable, married his employer's widow, and took over the business. Moving on to London, he set himself up as a bookseller and publisher and proved that though the streets were not paved with gold there was wealth to be made by an enterprising tradesman. He was never Lord Mayor, but he got to own his coach. He died rich and founded a family.

James Prior, in the first major life of Oliver Goldsmith, published in 1837, said that Newbery was "known for his probity, good sense, and a benevolent disposition. His ingenuity and amiable qualities rendered him generally respected. Writers of the first character sought his acquaintance, and in his friendship not unfrequently found occasional alleviation of their most pressing wants." Goldsmith and Dr Johnson were among those who borrowed guineas from him in times of need. He was also a writer: "Newbery is a remarkable man," observed Dr Johnson, "for I know not whether he has written or read most books." But the greater part of his wealth almost certainly came from a parallel trade as a promoter of patent medicines, the most notable being the once-famous Dr James's Fever Powder, in which Horace

Walpole said he had such faith that he believed he would take it if the house were on fire.

If these were his sole claims to fame, Newbery's name would survive only in footnotes to the biographies of greater men, and possibly an occasional mention in books about his period. In fact, however, it is known to thousands of people all through the English-speaking world. Teachers, librarians, book-collectors and others who are interested in children's literature have heard of him, if only because of the award which bears his name: the John Newbery Medal, presented yearly since 1922 for the most distinguished American children's book of the year. His achievement was to establish the production of books for children as a permanent and serious part of the publishing trade, and in some degree to set the pattern for its development.

But he is not a familiar figure to the general reader. The present book arises from a belief that he deserves to be better known, both for what he did and as an engaging character in his own right. It tries to bring together most of what is known and is of interest in his life and work, and gives some examples of the title-pages and advertisements on which he exercised his considerable ingenuity, as well as of the woodcuts with which he decorated his pages.

The present volume will be largely but not solely concerned with the children's books. Newbery published a great deal of other material and had fingers in many pies. His story casts light on the social and cultural background of his day. He was a self-made and self-educated man, busily engaged in making a fortune by supplying the needs of the rising middle class to which he belonged: an entrepreneur with an eye on the main chance. Yet at the same time he was in his way a man of the Enlightenment, a force in popular education, and an influence in changing adult attitudes to the bringing-up of children.

The only existing biography of Newbery is *A Bookseller of*

the Last Century, published in 1885 by Charles Welsh, a member of the firm which succeeded to one of the Newbery businesses. Welsh's book, though lengthy, is lacking in much that one would like to know. A new biography would be well worth while, if the materials for supplying Welsh's deficiencies existed; unfortunately most of them do not.

We have virtually no information about Newbery's early life and not much about his marriage and his relationships with his children. We have intriguing glimpses of him in action — notably the genial essay by Dr Johnson and the malicious but lively sketch of the Newberys at Oxford by George Colman, both of which are included here — but not much access to the inner nature of the man. Newbery did not leave any record of his private thoughts and feelings. Though indications of his views on various topics can be gleaned from the books which he may have written and for which he was certainly responsible, there is little scope for a modern biographer.

Yet to reissue Welsh's book as it stands would not make sense either. Some of it is inaccurate, a great deal is rambling or redundant, and there are facts that Welsh does not appear to have known. He worked mainly from existing literary sources — references to Newbery in works by or about his contemporaries — reinforcing them with extracts from the records of the firm and with information about the remedies which Newbery marketed. His account of his subject's life and work takes him only to the end of Chapter 6 (his page 117 out of 366.) Then comes an autobiography of Newbery's son Francis, a person of no great distinction, from whose writings Welsh has already extracted most of the interesting bits for use earlier on. The rest of the book consists mainly of a bibliography of the publications of Newbery and his successors up to the year 1800: a piece of research outdated by Sydney Roscoe's *John Newbery and his successors 1740-1814: a bibliography*, published in 1973.

The present volume contains an edited version of Welsh's first six chapters; his bibliography and Francis Newbery's contribution have been dropped. I have felt free to cut or omit some passages that I felt were prolix or repetitive and have removed some of Welsh's notes, while adding a few of my own; but I have not inserted anything into the text except an occasional connecting word. Essentially the words are Welsh's (and those of the earlier authorities from whom he quotes.)

The essay by Dr Johnson, which shows its author at his most sprightly and entertaining, first appeared as No. 19 in *The Idler,* a series of papers contributed in 1758-60 to the *Universal Chronicle or Weekly Gazette.* It was reprinted verbatim in the course of Welsh's fourth chapter. I have extracted it to stand alone, as it deserves to do. Welsh either did not know or preferred not to mention George Colman's essay, which was No. 3 of *Terrae-Filius,* a satirical series published in 1763.

Newbery and his contemporaries usually capitalized nouns. But they were not consistent, and I have felt free to take some liberties when quoting. I have substituted the modern style in extended passages, where the frequency of capital letters might impede reading or merely look quaint, but have kept the old style unchanged in a few places where it seemed best to preserve the original appearance.

There is no known contemporary portrait of John Newbery. A book called *The Newberys in Six Generations,* privately published by a descendant, A. Le Blanc Newbery, in 1911, contains what appears to be a representation of him but does not indicate where it came from or who the artist was. The assumption must be that it was imagined, and it is not reproduced in this book. My guess is that Newbery was too busy and insufficiently vain to sit for a portrait.

Many people have helped me with ideas, information or comment. I wish particularly to thank Ethel Heins, for the generous and characteristic sharing of her knowledge of everything to do with children's literature; Brian Alderson, for sage advice and the loan of books; Linda and Robert Yeatman for their creative and enthusiastic participation as publishers; and Jill Paton Walsh as always.

I have benefited from the works listed in the Bibliography, particularly from Harvey Darton's *Children's Books in England;* Sydney Roscoe's *John Newbery and his Successors,* mentioned above; Mary Thwaite's introduction to her edition of *A Little Pretty Pocket-book*; Christopher Devlin's *Poor Kit Smart*; and John Ginger's biography of Oliver Goldsmith, *The Notable Man.* I am grateful for the facilities provided by the Cambridge University Library, the Victoria and Albert Museum, the Cambridge and Reading public libraries, the St Bride Printing Library, the Houghton Library at Harvard, and the American Antiquarian Society at Worcester, Massachusetts. I also wish to thank Mr Ronald Newbery for sharing with me the results of his research into family history and Mrs Lorna Fox for information about Ralph Newbery and the Newbery charity. No one but myself however is responsible for any errors.

The photograph of Waltham St Lawrence churchyard was taken by me. Pat Craddock redrew the map on page 155 from parts of R. Horwood's London map of 1799. The Newbery Medal is reproduced on page 161 by courtesy of the American Library Association. Other illustrations are from copies or facsimiles in private collections.

J.R.T.

Cambridge, 1994.

A MAN OF PARTS

John Rowe Townsend

Riddle-me-ree

from

FOOD *for the* MIND; *or,*
a New RIDDLE - BOOK

MY proper title I forfake,
   And often that of others take;
Sometimes a king in ftately pride,
With lofty majefty I ftride;
Sometimes with fprightly nymphs and
      fwaine,
I trip it o'er the flow'ry plains;
Sometimes I fleet aloft in air,
And oftentimes quite difappear :
In various fhapes I'm known to be,
And children often ftart at me.

(*Food for the Mind; or, a New Riddle-Book*,
compiled by "John the Giant-Killer, Esq.," was
published by John Newbery in 1758)

A *man of parts*

IN *Children's Books in England* (1932), Harvey Darton, the first serious historian of children's literature, referred to John Newbery as "Newbery the Conqueror" and the year 1744, when he published his first children's book, as "a date comparable to the 1066 of the older histories." Undoubtedly this was written with tongue in cheek, and there may be an echo of Newbery's own engaging impudence. (His *Lilliputian Magazine* had the modest aims of "amending the world, rendering the society of men more amiable, and re-establishing the virtues of the Golden Age," while the reader of *Goody Two-Shoes* was referred to "the Original Manuscript in the Vatican at Rome, and the Cuts by Michael Angelo.")

Darton had defined children's books as "printed works produced ostensibly to give children spontaneous pleasure, and not primarily to teach them, nor solely to make them good, nor to keep them *profitably* quiet (his italics)." The key word in this carefully qualified definition is "pleasure." Newbery's books, like those of many more recent publishers, did not offer pleasure solely for its own sake; it was well understood that to the adults who actually paid for the books it was a powerful recommendation that they should teach a child something useful or improve its character. But the idea that the book should amuse as well as improve its reader was the distinguishing characteristic of the eighteenth-century books for Little Masters and Misses of which John Newbery's are the prime examples.

Before this time, children's literature may be said to have a dual prehistory. On the one hand there was material which was story, and well known to children, but not intended specially for them: the ancient romances, ballads and folktales, surviving from the days before print but out of favour among educated adults, either scorned as peasant crudities or detested as immoral and dangerous to youth. On the other hand there were courtesy books, schoolbooks, and books of moral exhortation, which were meant for children but were not story and were in no way intended to amuse. And, just before Newbery's day, there were three great works which were not written for children but which became children's books by adoption or adaptation: John Bunyan's *Pilgrim's Progress* (1678), Daniel Defoe's *Robinson Crusoe* (1719) and Jonathan Swift's *Gulliver's Travels* (1726).

The intellectual force behind the new concept of combining instruction with amusement was that of the English philosopher John Locke (1632-1704). In his *Treatise upon Education* (1693), Locke suggested that children could be "cozened into a knowledge of their letters, be taught to read, without perceiving it to be anything but a sport, and play themselves into that which others are whipped for." He also thought that when a child had learned to read it should be given "some easy pleasant book" which would reward it for its trouble without "filling its head with useless trumpery."[1]

Locke lamented the shortage of such books, and Newbery was the most important, though not the first, of those who consciously moved in to fill it. Before him there were the shadowy figures of "J.G.", who published in 1694 *A Play-Book for Children,* "to allure them to read as soon as they

---

[1] Locke, *Treatise upon Education,* Sections 149, 156

can speak plain," and "T.W.", who issued in about 1702 *A Little Book for Little Children,* setting down *in a plain and pleasant way, directions for spelling and other remarkable matter. Adorn'd with cuts.* There was Thomas Boreman, publisher between 1740 and 1743 of a series of tiny volumes called *Gigantick Histories;* and there were others. But it was Newbery who first made the publishing of children's books a substantial and successful business.

He was a man of and for his time: the Age of Reason. The view of children as arriving in the world steeped in original sin was losing ground to the concept of the *tabula rasa,* the blank page waiting to be written on. (The Wordsworthian picture of the child who comes into the world trailing clouds of glory, only to have the prison-house close around it, was still in the future.) It was also, in Britain, an age of consolidation after the turbulence of the previous century. The so-called Glorious Revolution of 1688 had established parliamentary government; life was becoming more settled and more domestic; the middle class was expanding and taking on some of the characteristics of a mass market. Children were beginning to be seen as persons with their own needs and interests, not merely as embryonic adults.

The new middle class was interested in self-improvement and in the education of its children, if only as a means to advancement. This was the opportunity that Newbery saw and seized. He could well be described as an educational publisher. He brought out many instructional books, both for adults and children: histories, dictionaries, letter-writers, and a kind of pocket general education in *The Circle of the Sciences,* issued in a series of small volumes between 1745 and 1748. Pocket books were in vogue; it was not by chance that his first title to be published in London, and first book for children, was called *A Little Pretty Pocket-Book.* Another pioneering innovation was a magazine for children, *The Lilliputian Magazine*, which ran for three numbers in 1751 and 1752. This was said on the title page to be "printed for T. Carnan at Mr Newbery's" (Carnan, then a very young man, was Newbery's stepson) but there is evidence that it was planned and paid for by Newbery. It was clearly not successful as a periodical, but was reprinted as a book, in which form it remained in print for many years.

Newbery owned or had shares in many publishing enterprises, including at least three newspapers, all small by modern standards. Alongside these ventures, he developed the patent medicine business which brought him a large part of his growing wealth. He was an astute advertiser and a master of the art of the puff. His books and medicines were frequently referred to in the pages of his own publications; Goody Two-Shoes's father, notoriously, died of a violent fever in a place where Dr James's Powder (the star performer among Newbery's nostrums) "was not to be had." His success in his various fields of endeavour may be put down to a gift for spotting and satisfying a growing market, helped by clever promotion. "Trade and Plumb-Cake for ever, Huzza!" was an appropriate slogan for one whose trade brought him an amplitude of plum-cake.

But there was more to it than that. Commercial though he was, Newbery was a man of the Enlightenment. He was an admirer of "the great Mr Locke," who is thus referred to, and quoted as an authority, in the foreword to the *Little Pretty Pocket-Book*. This foreword, addressed to "the parents, guardians and nurses in Great Britain and Ireland," and remarkably progressive in tone, makes it clear that the expected readership is middle-class:

> The grand design in the nurture of children is to make them *strong, hardy, healthy, virtuous, wise and happy*; and these good purposes are not to be obtained without some care and management in their infancy.
> Would you have your child *strong*, take care of your nurse; let her be a prudent woman, one that will give him what meat and drink is necessary, and such only as affords a good

A Little Pretty
P O C K E T - B O O K,
Intended for the
INSTRUCTION and AMUSEMENT
OF
LITTLE MASTER *TOMMY*,
AND
PRETTY MISS *POLLY*.
With Two Letters from
J A C K the G I A N T - K I L L E R ;
AS ALSO
A BALL and PINCUSHION;
The Use of which will infallibly make *Tommy*
a good Boy, and *Polly* a good Girl.

To which is added,
A LITTLE SONG-BOOK,
BEING
A *New Attempt* to teach Children the Use of
the *English Alphabet*, by Way of Diversion.

L O N D O N:
Printed for J. NEWBERY, at the *Bible and Sun*
in St. *Paul's Church-Yard*, 1767.
[Price Six-pence bound.]

A Little Pretty Pocket-Book: frontispiece and title-page of a 1767
edition. Earlier editions have almost entirely disappeared

nutriment, not salt meats, rich tarts, sauces, wine, &c., a
practice too common among some indulgent people. She must
also let the child have due exercise; for 'tis this that gives life
and spirits, circulates the blood, strengthens the sinews, and
keeps the whole machinery in order.

Would you have a hardy child, give him common diet only,
cloath him thin, let him have good exercise, and be as much
exposed to hardships as his natural constitution will admit . . .
Keep him, as much as possible, from physic, for physic is to the
body as arms to the state; both are necessary, but neither to be
used but in cases of emergency and danger. [An interesting
view, coming from a vendor of proprietary medicines.]

Would you have a virtuous son, instil into him the principles
of morality early, and encourage in him the practice of those
excellent rules by which whole societies, states, kingdoms and
empires are knit together. Take heed what company you intrust

him with, and be sure always to set him a good example yourself.

Would you have a wise son, teach him to reason early. Let him read, and make him understand what he reads. . . Let him study mankind; show him the springs and hinges on which they move; teach him to draw consequences from the actions of others; and if he should hesitate or mistake, you are to set him right. But then take care to do it in such a manner as to forward his enquiries, and pave this his grand pursuit with pleasure. . .

Happiness and misery have their source from the passions: if, in the midst of the greatest affluence, we are always repining, and think ourselves poor and miserable, we are so; and the beggar in the straw, who is content and thinks he has sufficient, is rich and happy. The whole matter subsists in the mind and the constitution: Subdue therefore your children's passions; curb their tempers, and make them subservient to the rules of reason. And this is not to be done by chiding, whipping, or severe treatment, but by reasoning and mild discipline. . .

> Children, like tender osiers, take the bow,
> And as they first are fashion'd, always grow. (DRYDEN.)

> 'Tis education forms the tender mind;
> Just as the twig is bent, the tree's inclined. (POPE.)

Newbery was always interested in education and science: the *Circle of the Sciences* was a remarkable achievement for its time in popular education, and one of his most successful books was an exposition by one Tom Telescope of *The Newtonian System of Philosophy*. Of this work, Professor J.H. Plumb has observed (in an essay on "The first flourishing of children's books" in Gerald Gottlieb's *Early children's books and their illustration*) that "it is crystal-clear, the examples exceptionally apposite, and its attitude to the universe, to philosophy, to humanity, and to the natural sciences would have drawn prolonged cheers from the Encyclopedists.

"Hence it is not only a brilliantly produced book for adolescent children, but it also gives us a novel insight in how the ideas of the Enlightenment were being disseminated through society."

The *Lilliputian Magazine* is introduced by "a dialogue between a Gentleman and the Author" in which the Author explains his design to sow in the minds of children, "by way of *history* and *fable,* the seeds of polite literature, and to teach them *the great grammar of the universe;* I mean, *the knowledge of men and things."* He declares that he will "not be afraid of a little expense" and goes on:

In fine, I shall give my young pupils as much for threepence one month as I apprehend they will be able to learn before the beginning of another . . . I don't in the least doubt but there are gentlemen and ladies enough who will encourage the undertaking by purchasing the numbers as they come out, either for their own children or their poor neighbours . . . You'll be pleased to consider, Sir, that the largest book is not always the best, and that books of this sort are to be made as cheap as possible; for there are a great many poor people in

The little k *Play.*   *The great* I *Play.*

BASE-BALL.   CRICKET.

THE *Ball* once ſtruck off,
   Away flies the *Boy*
To the next deſtin'd Poſt,
   And then Home with Joy.

THIS Leſſon obſerve,
   When you play at *Cricket,*
Catch *All* fairly out,
   Or bowl down the *Wicket.*

MORAL.   MORAL.

Thus *Britons* for Lucre
   Fly over the Main;
But, with Pleaſure tranſported,
   Return back again.

This Maxim regard,
   Now you're in your Prime;
Look ere 'tis too late;
   By the Fore-lock take *Time.*

TRAP-   C 3   STOOL-

Pages from *A Little Pretty Pocket-Book*

His Majesty's dominions who would not be able to purchase it at a larger price, and yet these are the King's subjects, and, in their station, as much to be regarded as the rest.

In spite of such ambitions, the Newbery children's books have an air of cheerful amiability, of humour and good-humour, that convince one of their publisher's enjoyment of what he was doing and affection for his customers. It was surely more than a sales gimmick when he described himself to child readers as "their old friend in St Paul's Churchyard." The dedication of *Goody Two-Shoes* is "to all Young Gentlemen and Ladies who are good or intend to be good." A late Newbery book, *The Fairing, or, a Golden Toy for Children of all Sizes and Denominations,* presumes on old acquaintance and has as its dedication: "To the True and Genuine Lovers of Noise, This Book, which was calculated for their Amusement and written for their Use, is most humbly inscribed by YOU KNOW WHO." With their inviting covers of flowered and gilt Dutch paper, the little books sold in their thousands, both in Newbery's lifetime and after his death. They were imported and later pirated in large numbers in post-revolutionary America, most notably by Isaiah Thomas of Worcester, Massachusetts, who adapted Newbery's phrase and addressed himself to the children as "their old friend in Worcester." In both countries, however, the books are now extremely rare.

◇

Welsh's characterization of Newbery is external, based on the testimony of contemporaries. The consensus among these is clear. It is agreed that he was energetic, optimistic, and benevolent — though his benevolence was not on a scale to impede him in amassing a fortune. But Welsh made no attempt to explore his emotional make-up, and indeed had no information on which to do so. From the little Newbery wrote in his own person (such as the preface to *Giles Gingerbread,* quoted later in this essay) we can get some impression of his views and outlook, which appear to have been liberal in a down-to-earth way. Rather more can be deduced about his private character from known facts about his family life.

Newbery was employed as a young man by William Carnan, a printer in Reading, and when Carnan died married his widow. Such a marriage was a time-honoured solution to the problem of a tradesman's early death, since it benefited all concerned. The employee was promoted, the widow and children provided for, and the continuance of the business assured. (In this case, however, marriage was not obligatory to secure the succession, as Newbery and Carnan's brother Charles, a linen-draper, were in fact Carnan's heirs.) Mrs Newbery was, according to her son Francis, "a most amiable and worthy woman" who "ever sacrificed her own enjoyments and devoted her time to the promotion of the happiness of others." These are somewhat standard terms of praise; a dutiful son could hardly say less. But the most pleasant passage in Francis Newbery's otherwise uninspiring memoir tells how, twelve years after his father's death, Francis invited a few friends to a housewarming at his spanking new house-cum-warehouse on the north-east side of St Paul's, and Dr Johnson was one of the party.

He was in high good humour, and rendered himself extremely agreeable to the company. He was particularly pleased on meeting our author's [Francis's] mother, not having seen her since the death of her husband, of whom he spoke with great affection and regard as an old and early friend. Amongst other reminiscences, our author's mother reminded Dr J. how much he had affronted her son by desiring him to give his fiddle to the first beggarman he met. . . Soon after this meeting, in the month of January (1780), our author's mother departed this life after a short illness, aged 73.

Welsh does not mention that Mary Newbery was a Catholic, of old recusant stock. She was the daughter of Martin Hounshill, a brazier, of Ringwood, Hampshire; her

Frontifpeice

Lecture on Matter &c. Motion?

THE
Newtonian System
OF
PHILOSOPHY

Adapted to the Capacities of young GENTLEMEN and LADIES, and familiarized and made entertaining by Objects with which they are intimately acquainted:

BEING
The Subſtance of SIX LECTURES read to the LILLIPUTIAN SOCIETY,

By TOM TELESCOPE, A.M.

And collected and methodized for the Benefit of the Youth of theſe Kingdoms,

By their old Friend Mr. NEWBERY; in *St. Paul's Church Yard*;

Who has alſo added Variety of Copper-Plate Cuts, to illuſtrate and confirm the Doctrines advanced.

O Lord, how manifold are thy Works! In Wiſdom haſt thou made them all, the Earth is full of thy Riches.
Young Men and Maidens, Old Men and Children, praiſe the Lord. PSALMS.

LONDON,
Printed for J. NEWBERY; at the BIBLE and SUN, in St. Paul's Church Yard. 1761.

The *Newtonian System of Philosophy*: frontispiece and title-page

brother, also Martin Hounshill, was ordained priest in 1742 and was imprisoned during the '45 rebellion. Penal laws against Catholicism had not yet been repealed, and although they were no longer rigorously enforced a common informer could still win an award of £100 by "discovering" a priest. John Newbery seems to have been solidly Protestant, but clearly had no time for religious bigotry. Christopher Devlin, in his biography of the poet Christopher Smart, who married Newbery's stepdaughter Anna Maria, says of the Newbery household:

According to the custom prevalent at that time in marriages of mixed religion, the boys were brought up in their father's persuasion, the girls in their mother's. Thus Thomas and John Carnan [Newbery's stepsons] were Protestants, Anna Maria was

(115)

ture ; for by a due temperament of thofe two oppofite qualities moft of her productions are formed.

What we call *heat* is occafioned by the agitation of the infenfible parts of the body that produces in us that fenfation ; and when the parts of a body are violently agitated, we fay, and indeed we feel, that body is *hot* ; fo that that which to our fenfation is *heat*, in the objeft is nothing but *motion*. Hey-day, fays Lady *Caroline*, what fort of Philofophy is this ? Why, Madam, fays Sir *Harry*, this is a pofition which has been laid down by thefe airy Gentlemen for a long time, but which never has been proved by experiment. Take care, Baronet, fays the Marquis, or you'll forfeit all pretenfions to Philofophy. The forfeiture, my Lord, is made already, fays the Philofopher ; Sir *Harry* has been bold enough to deny that which experience every day confirms for truth. If what we call Heat is not motion, or occafioned by the motion of bodies, how came my Lord's mill to take fire the other day, when it was running round without a proper fupply of corn ? And how came your poft-chariot to fire while running down *Breakneck-hill*, Sir *Harry* ? Confider, there was nobody with a torch under the axle-tree ;

Chariot fired by Motion

The Newtonian System of Philosophy: inside pages

a Catholic. Newbery seems to have followed the same custom; his little daughter Mary, born about 1742, was evidently brought up like her mother, for she later married a Catholic wine merchant, Michael Power.

Newbery was a good husband and a good father; he did not let religious differences cloud his family relations; in his will of 1762 he left money to his brother-in-law Martin, the priest, as well as to his Hounshill sisters-in-law. Under his sturdy protection his wife and stepdaughter were safe in the discreet practice of their proscribed religion.[1]

Smart, a highly gifted man and for a time a Fellow of Pembroke College, Cambridge, met Newbery in about 1750,

---

[1] Christopher Devlin, *Poor Kit Smart*, p. 63

was published by him, and edited for him a publication entitled *The Midwife,* conducted for two years by an imaginary and slightly sinister personage called Mary Midnight. Smart soon fell deeply in love with Anna Maria, whom he described in a poem as his "lass with the golden locks":

> Than the swan in the brook she's more dear to my sight,
> Her mien is more stately, her breast is more white,
> Her lips are like rubies, all rubies above,
> Which are fit for the language and labour of love;
> At the park in the mall, at the play in the box
> My lass bears the bell with her golden locks.

The story is told in Robert Surtees's *History of Durham* in what appear to be the words of Smart's and Anna Maria's daughter Elizabeth, still alive when Surtees was writing:

> The family were residing at Canonbury House, Islington, where Smart was a constant visitor. An intimacy, which soon ripened into affection, arose between him and Anna Maria Carnan, daughter of Mrs Newbery by her first husband. A clandestine marriage took place, without the consent of Mr Newbery, whose favour however was soon conciliated, and Smart was immediately established at Canonbury House, where he pursued his literary labours for several years.

Smart seems to have been happy there: "I bless God for my retreat at Canbury, as it was the place of nativity of my children." Elizabeth, who became Mrs Le Noir de la Brosse, a writer of some note in her day, also remembered it in later years with nostalgia. She wrote in one of her *Miscellaneous Poems* (1826), quoted by Christopher Devlin in his biography of Smart:

> Ah, still in fancy's eyes are seen
> The stately elms that formed its screen;
> Where my good grandsire, loved, caressed,
> Watched the old magpye build her nest,
> Or marked in distance just descried

The small white vessels smoothly glide,
As hills, half-veiled in aether blue,
Pointed old Thames's course to view.[1]

The "good grandsire" can only have been John Newbery.
Unfortunately, about three years after the marriage, Smart
had the first of the bouts of religious mania, interspersed
apparently with drunkenness, which caused him to spend
much of his remaining life in madhouses and to die in a
debtor's prison. He became violently opposed to Catholicism
and referred to his wife as "the Moabitish woman"
("Moabite" was a pejorative Puritan term for Roman
Catholics). His marriage and relationship with the Newberys
broke up; Anna Maria took refuge for a time with his sister
and her husband in Dublin. In 1762 Newbery set her up in
business at the *Reading Mercury*, which her father had
formerly owned and which she ran successfully for many
years as Anna Maria Smart and Company (later Smart and
Cowslade.)

Newbery was clearly a family man who believed in
keeping things in the family. His will contained bequests to
numerous relatives. He took his stepson Thomas Carnan and
his nephew Francis Newbery into the firm, and wanted the
bookselling business to be continued jointly by them and his
son Francis. (Confusion between the two Francis Newberys
began in their own day and has continued ever since. Francis
the nephew had in fact already branched out on his own
when John Newbery died, and took no part in the
partnership of Newbery & Carnan.)

As a father, John Newbery may have been excessively
indulgent; he supported Francis the son for five years of
study, or possibly idleness, at Oxford and Cambridge, in
which time Francis did not take any degree. As a husband,

---

[1] Elizabeth Smart Le Noir, *Miscellaneous Poems*, 1826, quoted by Devlin,
p.72.

no doubt he had his drawbacks. Johnson's essay, supported by other testimony and the multiplicity of Newbery's enterprises, makes it clear that he lived in an endless bustle of activity. Mary Newbery may well have been a business widow. But Newbery was industrious, an excellent provider, and presumably faithful: the lifestyle of Jack Whirler cannot have left much time for dalliance.

In a Ph.D. thesis for the University of California, Berkeley, in 1972, J.D.C. Buck suggests that

[the] sense of an autocratic and demanding though highly benevolent father is crucial to the understanding of Newbery and his career. The paternal role is one which he played not only for his family but also for the hacks in his employ. . . He treated his writers as though they too were his children. The role of provider was merely extended from these relationships to the more general one of uncle to all the children who bought or read his books.

Authors and other hard-pressed professionals may reflect ruefully that it was Newbery the businessman who became rich, not Johnson, Goldsmith or Smart, the men of genius. But life was ever thus. The men of genius would have been worse off, not better, if Newbery had not existed; the people who learned from his publications and the children who enjoyed the little books would have been poorer.

◇

There are some unsolved mysteries, however, surrounding the life of John Newbery. The first question is: who actually *wrote* all those little books? The Newbery books for children are either anonymous or have obviously fictional authors (Thomas Trip, Tommy Trapwit, Tom Telescope et al.). Anonymous authorship was not unusual at the time; the "moral right" to be identified as the author of one's work was not developed until centuries later.

It must be said that in this case there is not much posthumous glory attached to the authorship. With one or two exceptions such as *The Newtonian System of Philosophy,* the Newbery books are more notable for their title-pages than for their texts. That the books for the instruction and amusement of little masters and misses were remembered affectionately in later life by such men of letters as Charles Lamb, Robert Southey and Leigh Hunt says more about the absence of competition than about the virtues of the books themselves. Story and verse elements seem unimpressive to modern eyes, and the instructional intentions all too evident. Good children are rewarded; bad children come to bad ends. Goodness means being obedient, dutiful and honest, rising early, saying your prayers, telling no lies, learning your book, being kind to others and to animals. You are allowed a little naughtiness if you are sorry afterwards. A good little boy may hope to become a fine man and ride a fine horse; a good little girl to become a fine woman and ride in a fine coach. Rewards are not entirely material, however: if you are truthful, honest etc you will have a good conscience and will be loved. There are occasional lively touches, and at least the books are child-friendly. "Be good or nobody will love you" is a less daunting message than "Be good or you will go to hell."

There is a tendency to attribute well-known anonymous works to well-known writers. The name most often associated with the Newbery books is that of Oliver Goldsmith, who did a great deal of hack-work for Newbery; and the best-known attribution to Goldsmith is that of the best-known Newbery title, *Goody Two-Shoes.* But there is no real evidence to support it. The case for Goldsmith rests partly on stylistic grounds — which do not seem to me to be strong; I cannot believe that Goldsmith would not have made a better job of it — and partly on the supposed similarity of sentiments between the first chapter of *Goody Two-Shoes* and Goldsmith's poem *The Deserted Village,* published five years later. Goody's father is made homeless when his landlord Sir

Timothy Gripe combines a dozen farms into one, a practice which the author condemns as one which "in the end must reduce the common people to a state of vassalage." But this was not a unique sentiment, and Goldsmith's targets in *The Deserted Village* are much broader.

The "introduction" to *Goody,* by "the Editor," has a teasing passage, following the account of the landlord's and the large farmer's villainies:

> But what, says the Reader, can occasion all this? Do you intend this for children, Mr NEWBERY? — Why, do you suppose this is written by Mr NEWBERY, Sir? This may come from another hand. This is not the book, Sir, mentioned in the title, but the introduction to that book; and it is intended, Sir, not for those sort of children, but for children of six feet high, of which, as my friend has justly observed, there are many millions in the kingdom. . .

This leaves us in the dark, as it was meant to do. Are there separate figures of Author and Editor, or should we (as I am inclined to think) detect Mr Newbery himself in both guises? He was a farmer's son with farming relatives: closer to the land, in fact, than Goldsmith.

There is a rival attribution which would ascribe *Goody Two-Shoes* to the brothers Giles and Griffith Jones, literary hacks of the day. This appears to rest on the claim made in a *New Biographical Dictionary* published in 1794 by Stephen Jones, Giles Jones's son. The claim was energetically pushed by Giles's grandson, John Winter Jones, principal librarian at the British Museum from 1866 to 1878, but I know of no evidence to support it beyond the assertions of the Joneses. It has been observed, with no great relevance, that at the end of the book Margery Two-Shoes becomes Lady Jones.

There are in fact strong and obvious grounds for guessing that Newbery himself was the author of many, perhaps all, of what were always known as "Mr Newbery's little books." Johnson, who said he did not know whether Newbery had

important Business, and the first House we came to was Farmer *Wilson's.* See here it is.

Here *Margery* stopped, and ran up to the Door, *Tap, tap, tap.* Who's there? Only little goody *Two-Shoes,* answered *Margery,* come to teach *Billy.* Oh Little *Goody,* says Mrs. *Wilson,* with Pleasure in her Face, I am glad to see you, *Billy* wants you

to flap at the Window, *Wow, wow, wow,* says Jumper, and attempted to leap up and open the Door, at which the Children were surprized; but Mrs. *Margery* knowing what it was, opened the Casement, as *Noah* did the Window of the Ark, and drew in *Tom* Pidgeon with a Letter, and see here he is.

As soon as he was placed on the Table, he walked up to little *Sally.* and

Bow wow, wow, says the Dog at the Door. Sirrah, says his Mistress, what do you bark at Little *Two-Shoes.* Come in *Madge*; here, *Sally* wants you sadly, she has learned all her Lesson. Then out came the little one : So *Madge!* says she; so *Sally!* answered the other, have you learned your Lesson? Yes, that's what I have, replied the little one in the

sent *Gaffer Goosecap,* a busy Fellow in other People's Concerns, to find out Evidence against her. This Wiseacre happened to come to her School, when she was walking about with the Raven on one Shoulder, the Pidgeon on the other, the Lark on her Hand, and the Lamb and the Dog by her Side; which indeed made a droll Figure, and so surprized the Man, that he cried out,

a Witch !

Pages (not consecutive) from *Goody Two-Shoes*

read or written more books, and Goldsmith, in the famous passage about the philanthropic bookseller who had written so many little books for children, were referring to someone they both knew well, and their testimony carries more weight than can later speculations.

There are other indicators which, while falling short of proof, point in the direction of Newbery's own authorship. One of them is that early example of the Amazing Free Offer, the advertisement for *Nurse Truelove's New Year's Gift*, "printed for the author, who has ordered these books to be given gratis to all little boys and girls, at the Bible and Sun in St Paul's Churchyard, they paying for the binding, which is only twopence each book." The usual Newbery imprint was "printed for J. Newbery, at the Bible and Sun in St Paul's Churchyard," and certainly it was Newbery who gave the orders there, so the advertisement would suggest that he was the author. (On the other hand, Newbery was not on oath in framing his advertisements.) Then there is the preface to *Giles Gingerbread*:

> The Reader perhaps may be so unreasonable as to expect an account of the birth, parentage and country of our hero. If he does, I can assure him he will be disappointed. There are circumstances which he has no right to be informed of; for a good man may be born any how and anywhere; of any parents and in any country.
>
> Whether you, gentle Reader, were born at my native place, Waltham, where the frogs sing like nightingales, or at any other place, you may be as wise and as honest as I am.
>
> If a man is a good man, and an honest man, it is no matter where he was born; and if those who have lately made so much noise about country and party had been scholars to Gaffer Gingerbread, he would have knocked their heads together for being such boobies.

This was undoubtedly written by Newbery, whose birthplace was Waltham St Lawrence, and although signed by "the Bookseller" it has an authorial air.

The most striking feature of the Newbery children's books is the strong family likeness that runs through them for all the 23 years in which John Newbery was in business in St Paul's Churchyard. A distinctive personality is visible in the production, especially in the style and content of title-pages, and extends to the way they were advertised and promoted. The main reason for feeling unsure that Newbery was his own author is that he was so continually busy that it is hard to see how he could have found the time. But George Colman's essay mocks Newbery, *inter alia,* as bookseller-author going around with his latest manuscript in his hand. And even if he did not write the books, or all of them, himself, there is no doubt that his was the originating and the guiding spirit. His successors, though they tried, were unable to maintain the Newbery style.

◇

Then there is the question of what was paid to Goldsmith, and by whom, for *The Vicar of Wakefield,* published in 1767 by Francis Newbery the nephew but apparently financed at least in part by his uncle. John Newbery has been accused in later times of dealing meanly with Goldsmith over this book. Sums of twenty, forty and sixty pounds (or guineas) were mentioned respectively by William Cooke in 1793, Sir John Hawkins in 1787, and Johnson as reported by Boswell in the *Life of Johnson,* published in 1791. Welsh's discovery of a payment of twenty-one pounds to Goldsmith by the printer Benjamin Collins of Salisbury four years before actual publication raised a further question: could Goldsmith possibly have sold his work twice over to different people? But meanness would have been uncharacteristic of Newbery's dealings with Goldsmith, who was paid for more work than he actually did and who, according to Francis Newbery the son, owed his father the then-large sum of two hundred pounds when John Newbery died. Dishonesty in Goldsmith seems equally unlikely; he often had trouble in paying his debts but did not engage in double-dealing. And Collins would have found him out, for the imprint on the first edition was "Salisbury: Printed by B. Collins for F. Newbery in Paternoster Row."

This tangled matter seems to me to be satisfactorily sorted out by Austin Dobson in his *Life of Oliver Goldsmith* (1888). It appears that the book was bought in three equal shares by Collins, John Newbery and William Strahan, the sums referred to representing one, two and three shares in different contexts. The total payment of sixty pounds or guineas was reasonable enough, in the money terms of the day: as Welsh shows (page 75), the book took eight years to show a profit, and Collins sold his share for a fraction of what he had paid. Why the book was published by Francis the nephew, round the corner, when John Newbery was still alive and active at the Bible and Sun is unclear, but Austin Dobson refers in another context to "some occult arrangement between the Newberys," which seems sufficient explanation. Later, to add to the confusion, the book passed to Carnan and Francis the son.

The author of a memoir of Goldsmith of which there is a copy in the Cambridge University Library, lacking date or title page but from internal evidence written within a few years after Goldsmith's death, tells the Johnson version of the story and names Newbery — obviously meaning John — as the buyer, but says he "seems not to have been very sanguine in his hopes for the novel. . . for he kept the MS by him near three years unprinted; his ready purchase of it probably was in the way of a benefaction to its distressed author rather than under any idea of profit by the publication." This author refers to Newbery as "one of the best judges and most liberal rewarders of literary merit."

◇

The last question is a non-literary one: what about Dr James's Powder? It was assiduously sold by John Newbery and his descendants and was a cornerstone of the family fortunes. The epitaph on Newbery's tomb at Waltham St Lawrence praises the "sagacity that discerned and skill that introduced the most powerful discovery in the annals of medicine." Horace Walpole was one of a great many who had faith in it. Henry Fielding, in his novel *Amelia,* declared that in almost any country but England the powder would have brought "public honours and awards" to his "worthy and ingenious friend Dr James." But there were some who thought it too powerful to be at large, especially after the death of Goldsmith, seven years after John Newbery, in 1774.

An apothecary called William Hawes, who attended Goldsmith in his last illness, wrote that Goldsmith was suffering from violent head pains and a high pulse-rate and, in spite of medical advice that "his complaint appeared to be more a nervous affection than a febrile disease," insisted against strong opposition on taking large and repeated doses of Dr James's Powder. This resulted in violent vomiting and purging which led to his death. Hawes said that he had seen several cases "wherein this noted fever-powder had proved highly injurious; which must generally be the consequence when an antimonial medicine, very violent frequently in its operation, has become so universally fashionable as to be administered in almost all feverish complaints, and in all stages of fevers, and be often suffered to be given at the discretion of old women, or at least by those who cannot have the smallest pretensions to medical knowledge."[1]

This calamity does not seem to have damaged the reputation of the famous powder, which was prescribed for King George III in his attack of mania in November 1788.

---

[1] William Hawes, *An account of the late Dr Goldsmith's illness, so far as relates to the exhibition of Dr James's Powder, together with Remarks on the use and abuse of powerful medicines in the beginning of fevers and other acute diseases,* by William Hawes, apothecary: 3rd edition, printed for W. Brown and others, London, 1774.

(From what we now know about the King's malady —
porphyrism — it is not surprising that it failed to cure him.)
Its main ingredients appear to have been phosphate of lime
and oxide of antimony. Though now no longer in
production, it flourished through several generations of the
Newbery family.[1]

John Newbery himself may have been a firm believer in
the powder and in Greenough's Tincture for the Teeth, as
well as in Daffy's Elixir, the "Alterative Pill" for the King's
Evil, and many other remarkable remedies. I find it hard to
suppose that he was a conscious peddler of worthless cures;
if he was, it is remarkable that quacks are satirised in
Newbery publications — as, for instance, is a fairground
mountebank in *The Fairing*. Most likely he justified the sale
of these profitable lines with the belief that they were as
effective as anything else that could be bought. Newbery was
regarded by his contemporaries as notably honest. In his will
he described himself as "bookseller," from which we can
deduce that his books were closer to his heart than his
medicines. It is because of the little books for children that
he is remembered, and, on the precept that a person should
be judged by the best of his deeds, he is entitled to be
honoured. He was a great man in a small way.

---

[1] See the second part of my note on "The inheritors," pp. 157-159.

JACK WHIRLER

Samuel Johnson, Ll.D.

Riddle-me-ree

from

F O O D *for the* M I N D; *or,*
a New R I D D L E - B O O K

'THE world I view in little fpace
I'm reftlefs, ever changing place,
Nothing I eat, but by my pow'r,
Procure what all mankind devour.

Jack Whirler

[This was No. 19 of *The Idler*, a series of essays which Johnson contributed from 1758 to 1760 to a newspaper called the *Universal Chronicle, or Weekly Gazette*. It has always been accepted, and was confirmed by Newbery's son Francis (see pp. 83-84), that the original of Jack Whirler was Newbery.

As Newbery had launched the paper and was a part-proprietor, Johnson may be said to have been poking good-humoured fun at his employer. Newbery was a tolerant man; Welsh says he threatened to repay Johnson in kind, but obviously he never got around to it. When the newspaper ceased publication, *The Idler* was reissued in book form.]

SOME of those ancient sages that have exercised their abilities in the enquiry after the Supreme Good have been of opinion that the highest degree of earthly happiness is quiet; a calm repose both of mind and body, undisturbed by the sight of folly or the noise of business, the tumults of public commotion or the agitations of private interest; a state in which the mind has no other employment but to observe and regulate her own motions, to trace thought from thought, combine one image with another, raise systems of science, and form theories of virtue.

To the scheme of these solitary speculatists it has been justly objected that if they are happy they are happy only by being useless; that mankind is one vast republic where every individual receives many benefits from the labour of others, which, by labouring in his turn for others, he is obliged to repay; and that where the united efforts of all are not able to exempt all from misery, none have a right to withdraw from their talk of vigilance, or to be indulged in idle wisdom or solitary pleasures. It is common for controvertists, in the heat of disputation, to add one position to another till they reach the extremities of knowledge, where truth and falsehood lose their distinction. Their admirers follow them to the brink of absurdity, and then start back from each side towards the middle point. So it has happened in this great disquisition. Many perceive alike the force of the contrary arguments, find quiet shameful and business dangerous, and therefore pass their lives between them, in bustle without business and in negligence without quiet.

Among the principal names of this moderate set is that great philosopher JACK WHIRLER, whose business keeps him in perpetual motion, and whose motion always eludes his business; who is always to do what he never does, who cannot stand still because he is wanted in another place, and who is wanted in many places because he stays in none. Jack has more business than he can conveniently transact in one house; he has therefore one habitation near Bow Church and another about a mile distant. By this ingenious distribution of himself between two houses, Jack has contrived to be found at neither. Jack's trade is extensive, and he has many dealers; his conversation is sprightly, and he has many companions; his disposition is kind, and he has many friends.

Jack neither forbears pleasure for business nor omits business for pleasure, but is equally invisible to his friends and his customers; to him that comes with an invitation to a club and to him that waits to settle an account. When you call at his house, his clerk tells you that Mr Whirler has just stepped out, but will be at home exactly at two; you wait at a coffee-house till two, and then find that he has been at home and is going out again, but left word that he should be at the Half-Moon Tavern at seven, where he hopes to meet you.

At seven you go to the tavern. At eight in comes Mr Whirler to tell you that he is glad to see you, and only begs leave to run for a few minutes to a gentleman that lives near the Exchange, from whom he will return before supper can be ready. Away he runs to the Exchange to tell those who are waiting for him that he must beg them to defer the business till tomorrow, because his time is come at the Half-Moon.

Jack's cheerfulness and civility rank him among those whose presence never gives pain, and whom all receive with fondness and caresses. He calls often on his friends to tell them he will come again tomorrow; on the morrow he comes again to tell them how an unexpected summons hurries him away. When he enters a house his first declaration is that he cannot sit down; and so short are his visits that he seldom appears to have come for any other reason but to say he must go.

The dogs of Egypt, when thirst brings them to the Nile, are said to run as they drink for fear of the crocodiles. Jack Whirler always dines at full speed. He enters, finds the family at table, sits familiarly down, and fills his plate; but while the first morsel is in his mouth hears the clock strike and rises; then goes to another house, sits down again, recollects another engagement, has only time to taste the soup, makes a short excuse to the company, and continues through another street his desultory dinner.

But, overwhelmed as he is with business, his chief desire is to have still more. Every new proposal takes possession of his thoughts; he soon balances probabilities, engages in the project, brings it almost to completion, and then forsakes it for another, which he catches with the same alacrity, urges with the same vehemence, and abandons with the same coldness.

Every man may be observed to have a certain strain of lamentation, some peculiar theme of complaint on which he dwells in his moments of dejection. Jack's topic of sorrow is the want of time. Many an excellent design languishes in empty theory for want of time.

For the omission of any civilities, want of time is his plea to others; for the neglect of any affairs, want of time is his excuse to himself. That he wants time he sincerely believes, for he once pined away many months with a lingering distemper for want of time to attend his health.

Thus Jack Whirler lives in perpetual fatigue, without proportionate advantage, because he does not consider that no man can see all with his own eyes or do all with his own hands; that whoever is engaged in multiplicity of business must transact much by substitution and leave something to hazard, and that he who attempts to do all will waste his life in doing little.

A BOOKSELLER OF THE
LAST CENTURY

Charles Welsh

LUDGATE HILL IN THE LAST CENTURY.

(From the Picture by Marlow.)

A BOOKSELLER
OF THE LAST CENTURY

Being some Account of the Life of
John Newbery, and of the
Books he published,
with a Notice
of the later
Newberys

By *CHARLES WELSH*

Printed for *Griffith, Farran, Okeden & Welsh*, successors to
Newbery & Harris, at *the sign of the Bible and Sun*, West
Corner of St Paul's Churchyard, London; and *E. P.
Dutton & Co.*, New York, MDCCCLXXXV.

CHARLES WELSH, born in 1850, was a literary historian and bibliographer with a special interest in children's books and chapbooks. In 1881 he edited and wrote the introduction to a facsimile of *Little Goody Two-Shoes* for the publishing house of Griffith and Farran, successors to the business founded in 1767 by John Newbery's nephew Francis. (See section on *The Inheritors,* pages 154-157.) By 1885, when he wrote *A Bookseller of the Last Century,* Welsh was a partner in the firm, which had changed its name to Griffith, Farran, Okeden and Welsh. It continued in this style until 1891, when Welsh left. He went to the United States and continued to be active in the same field, editing a series of facsimiles of early books. He died in 1914, within a few days of the outbreak of World War I.

In the text that follows, Welsh's footnotes are indicated by the initial W and those that I have added by the initial T.

The frontispiece to Welsh's book is from a painting by William Marlow (1740-1813), an artist well known in his day.   J.R.T.

A BOOKSELLER OF THE
LAST CENTURY

CHAPTER I

Ancestors——The Newberie Charity——John Newbery's Birthplace——Early Days in Waltham St.Lawrence——Reading——Death of Carnan——The *Reading Mercury*——Marriage——A Business Tour——Schemes for Future Work——The Business at Reading——B.Collins of Salisbury——Removal to London.

ALTHOUGH John Newbery was the son of a small farmer, living in an obscure and remote Berkshire village, it is noticeable that he came of a stock which had been intimately associated with books. Ralph or Rafe Newberie (*sic*), from whom, according to a pedigree in the present family, he traced his descent, was one of the greatest publishers at the end of the sixteenth century, who had his printing house in Fleet Street, a little above the Conduit. He was Warden of the Stationers' Company in 1583, and Master in 1598 and in 1601; he gave a stock of books, and the privilege of printing, to be sold for the benefit of Christ's Hospital and Bridewell. His first book is dated 1560, and his name appears on many of the most important publications of his day, such as *Hakluyt's Voyages, Holinshead's Chronicles,* a handsome Latin Bible, in folio (by Junius, Tremellius, &c.), 1593, which he published in conjunction with George Bishop and R. Barker. Among other productions of his press may be noted

Eclogues, Epitaphs, &c., 1563; Stow's *Annals,* 1592 and 1601; *A Book of the Inuention of the Art of Nauigation,* London, 1578, quarto; *An Ancient Historie and Curious Chronicle,* London, 1578; *A Remonstrance, or plain detection of some of the faults and hideous Sores of such sillie Syllogismes and Impertinent allegations, out of Sundrie Pamphlets and Rhapsodies as are cobled up into a Book, intituled, A Demonstration of Discipline, etc.,* London, 1590. In the same year he printed, in Greek types, *Joannis Chrysostomi,* &c.

Ralph Newbery bequeathed a sum of £5 annually for the poor of the Parish of Waltham St Lawrence, Berkshire, which bequest is now known as the Bell Charity. This has been invested in a small cottage and a portion of waste land. The former has been converted into the village public house, the tenant of which is elected by the trustees of the Charity, the latter into an orchard; and the Charity now (1885) brings in about £50 per annum. It was to be distributed among "the poorest and the neediest" under certain stated conditions as to the occupier of the house and the apportionment of the money, and it has been for years given away in money at Christmas to the poorer parishioners selected at a meeting of the trustees, a small part of the income being retained for repairs.

It was in this same parish of Waltham St Lawrence that John Newbery first saw the light. He was the younger son of Robert Newbery, a small farmer in the village, and was born in the year 1713 — the parish registers containing the entry of his baptism on the July 9 in that year. The place is prettily situated five miles south-west of Maidenhead, and nine miles east of Reading. Lord Braybrooke, a descendant of the Sir Henry Neville upon whom the manor was bestowed by King Edward the Sixth, is the present proprietor. In 1801 the village was described as follows:— "Though now reduced to a few scattered houses, it is said to have been a place of remote antiquity and of much importance. Some of the buildings wear the appearance of having flourished in better times, and the ruins of many more are visible. The inhabitants assert that the houses were formerly very numerous; that they extended a considerable way on each side of the road, which, at the entrance to the village, passes under an arched gateway composed of large oak timbers. In a spacious field near was a Roman fortress, the site of which is still called Castle Acre, and it commands a delightful view over a very large extent of country."

I paid it a visit in the summer of 1885, and found it quiet and quaint enough. It consists of a few old and scattered houses, and contains about 500 inhabitants. Approaching it from Twyford, one passes, not through the arched gateway of oak timbers, which has long since disappeared, but through lanes flanked by rows of "immemorial elms," casting a deep and grateful shade; opposite the church, in the middle of the road, stands the village pound, all choked with weeds, guarded at each corner by massive old ivy-covered oaks. Close at hand is the village inn, the Bell, where, as we have said, the Ralph Newberie Charity is annually distributed. The ringing of the hammer on the anvil denoted the near presence of the village blacksmith and church bellringer, and this was the only sound that disturbed the drowsy quietude of this out-of-the-way little nook.

Hard by is the rectory, and in the churchyard I found the graves of the Newbery family, some of whom, to judge from the mural records, were evidently persons of distinction in the parish in times gone by.[1] Humphrey Newbery, "late an

---

[1] The Parish Registers contain the name from 1559 onwards, and for about two hundred years there is scarcely a page on which it does not appear. — W.

See also my note on the earlier Newberys in "Sidelights" (pp. 143-147.) — T.

Utter Barrester of Lincolns Inn, who for his greate learning and knowledge in the Lawes of this Land was much esteemed by them that knew him and his worth" lies buried here. He died in 1638. Here also is the tomb of that "religious gentlewoman," his wife, "whose pious care in a religious education of her children was one among many fruites of her godly life. She deceased in 1640. . . and on her right side sleepes her youngest daughter Dorothy, whose early wisdome and goodness was a presedent for riper yeares. . . She left this world in 1634."[1]

It was in this quiet village that John Newbery, afterwards the active, bustling and energetic London publisher, passed his boyhood, and here he received the ordinary education of a farmer's son, which could not, we imagine, have been very extensive or complete. However, we learn from an autobiography of his son, Francis Newbery, that he, "by his talents and industry, and a great love of books, had rendered himself a very good English scholar. His mind was too excursive to allow him to devote his life to the occupation of agriculture. He was anxious to be in trade, and at about the age of sixteen, as he was a very good accountant, and wrote an excellent hand, he engaged himself as an assistant in the house of one of the principal merchants in Reading, where his diligence and integrity soon established his character, while his agreeable manners and conversation, and information (for he pursued his studies in all his leisure hours) raised him into notice and esteem."

---

[1] On a warm June day in 1993, Waltham St Lawrence was still drowsing: a small quiet village at which three country lanes meet as if by chance. The pound, tidied up, remains the focal point; beside it are the fine old church and the still-flourishing Bell Inn, now somewhat up-market. There are a score or more of enviably attractive houses. In the churchyard, close to a great 300-year-old yew, is the tomb of John Newbery (see pages 81-82) with its inscription, now somewhat eroded, still exhorting passers-by to stay and contemplate his virtues. — T.

Reading at this period (about 1730) was not in the height of its prosperity, and there were few, if any, merchants there in those days. It must have been then, as now, exceedingly pretty in its surroundings, and being situated at the confluence of the Thames and the Kennet, and on the high road from London to Bristol, there would naturally be a considerable traffic by land and water. Its market was reported one of the best in England for all sorts of grain and other provisions, but the town had not developed its present [1885] mercantile importance, with its great Biscuit Factory, its Seed Stores and its Ironworks. Its fame at about that time seems to have been chiefly for the manufactures of cloth and of malt, both of which have long since ceased.

We are unable to ascertain who is the "merchant" particularly referred to by Francis Newbery, but we conclude that it was Wm. Carnan the printer, proprietor and editor of one of the earliest provincial newspapers, the *Reading Mercury and Oxford Gazette*,[1] for we find in the records at Somerset House that Wm. Carnan, printer of Reading, died in 1737, leaving all his property and his business to his brother Charles and to John Newbery, appointing them his executors. The *Reading Mercury* first appeared on July 8, 1723, and was said to have been started by Mr John Watts, one of the mayors of that city.[2] Wm. Carnan in 1736 printed an edition in folio of Ashmole's *History and Antiquities of Berkshire*, but we find no traces of his imprint elsewhere.

To return, however, to the future publisher, who was by this time about twenty-four years of age, and had no doubt

---

[1] Welsh's conclusion was wrong. Newbery "engaged himself" in 1730 to William Ayres, a predecessor of Carnan as proprietor and printer of the *Mercury*. See my note on "The *Reading Mercury*," pages 147-150. — T.

[2] Welsh was wrong again. Watts was an important local figure, but there is no evidence that he founded the *Mercury*. See the note referred to above. — T.

become familiar with the routine of the printing office. Not long after Carnan's death John Newbery began to pay his addresses to his widow, who was about six years older than himself, and was left with three young children. We must here again quote his son Francis, who says in the autobiography before cited: "His love of books and acquirements had peculiarly fitted him for conducting such a concern as the newspaper and printing business at Reading, and rendered him doubly acceptable to the object of his affections, who was indeed a most amiable and worthy woman. They were in due time united in wedlock, and what a field now opened to his active and expanded mind!"

Of this marriage there were three children: Mary, born in March 1740, who married in 1766 Mr Michael Power, a Spanish merchant, and left a numerous family, some of whom were afterwards connected with the business in St Paul's Churchyard; John, born in September 1741, who was, says Francis Newbery, a "boy of singular acuteness and sense, but he had the misfortune so to injure his spine by a fall down some stone steps when a child, that he died after a lingering illness, aged eleven years. Christopher Smart, the poet, celebrated his memory in the following very nervous and appropriate epitaph:—

> Henceforth be every tender fear supprest,
> Or let us weep for joy, that he is blest;
> From grief to bliss, from earth to heav'n removed,
> His mem'ry honour'd, as his life belov'd,
> That heart o'er which no evil e'er had power,
> That disposition sickness could not sour;
> That sense, so oft to riper years denied,
> That patience heroes might have own'd with pride!
> His painful race undauntedly he ran,
> And in the eleventh winter died A MAN.[1]

---

[1] This was originally published in *The Midwife*. — W.

The youngest, Francis, was born on July 6, 1743, and, as we shall see, succeeded, with others, to the business of which his father was then so busy in laying the foundations.

> "He speedily," continues Francis, "became thoroughly master of his business, which was carried on for three or four years longer, when he opened a house in London, for the more ready disposal of a variety of publications which were printed at Reading, and of which he was either the author or compiler."

Before removing to London, however, he went, in the year 1740, on a tour through England, apparently for the benefit of the business in Reading, which was rapidly becoming of a very miscellaneous character. An account of this trip is preserved in his Private Memorandum Book, in which is entered each day's journeyings, the miles he travelled, the inns at which he lay, and all the notable sights that were seen. The manufactures, products and characteristics of the various towns are also briefly noted.

He started from Reading on Wednesday, July 9, 1740, and went to London by coach, alighting at the White Horse in Fleet Street. Thence on to St Albans, Bedford, Leicester, Melton Mowbray and Grantham, to Lincoln. "Going from this place" (Grantham) "to Lincoln," he says, "you cross a delicious plain, in length about 22 miles, the breadth I know not; in the whole 22 miles there is but one village (called Ancaster), and that just at the entrance of the down. Here we were almost famished for want of liquour, being obliged to travel upwards of 20 miles on a sultry summer's day without a drop. The spirit moved my brother traveller to ask the Shepard (*sic*), but the inhospitable wretch would not spare one spoonful." Who the brother traveller was does not transpire; it was probably a chance acquaintance, as although the word "we" sometimes occurs, he seems to have been alone most of the time. At Hull he was much entertained by "the effigie of the Bonny Boatman," in a boat made of fish skins, which was brought there by "a merchant of Hull in his voyage from Greenland near 100 years ago." From Hull he went to York, Lancaster, Doncaster (where he received his first letter from his wife), Sheffield, Nottingham, &c.; to Darby (sic), where, says he, "there is another curious and very useful machine, viz., a Ducking Stool, for the benefit of scholding wives. A plan of this instrument I shall procure and transplant to Berkshire for the good of my native county. . . "

Chester, Liverpool, Birmingham, Manchester, where he is to receive letters from his wife, are visited and described. "At Leicester gaol," he says, "we saw one John Clark who lay condemn'd for robbing on the highway. He told us that the person hanged at York was not Turpin,[1] for that he had robbed with him (Turpin) between Colnbrook and Maidenhead and other places the last hard weather, that the person then hang'd was an accomplish of his and Turpin's, and that they engaged that which ever were catched should take on him the name of Turpin, and that Turpin and he supported that man (viz., Palmer) in York Castle and were present at his execution; and that Turpin and he (John Clark) waited 8 weeks to shoot a man on Epping Forest. But that Turpin was now living and had taken on him the name of Smith, and he kept an alehouse in the North of England." Captain Twyford, in his records of York Castle,[2] tells us that Turpin was hanged on April 17, 1739. One account of his execution declares that he was distinguished by the comeliness of his appearance. "But," says Captain Twyford, "he was not at all prepossessing, really having high broad cheekbones, a short visage, the face narrowed towards the chin and was much marked by the smallpox." We cannot

---

[1] Richard [Dick] Turpin (1706-39), a notorious highwayman. — T.

[2] *Records of York Castle*, by A.W. Twyford and Major A. Griffiths: Griffith & Farran London, 1880. — W.

imagine there is any doubt as to the identity of this malefactor, but it is curious to read these conflicting descriptions as to his personal appearance in connection with the statement made by the robber who lay in Leicester gaol.

This robber, according to the *Reading Mercury* of August 25, 1740, was capitally convicted for a long catalogue of crimes, including the robbing of his Grace the Duke of Marlborough's coach between Reading and Maidenhead of about £90, and the commission of 23 other robberies on the highway.

At Leicester, Newbery writes also, "Some time ago the cookmaid of this Inn (The Three Cranes), being married, was delivered of two children, which the good unexperienced woman took for boys, and therefore at the christening named them John and Joseph, but since the said christening *Nature* has suffered a surprising change or the *wise ones* were out in their Judgment, for the two boys are become two girls."

Engines at that time were evidently rare objects, for our traveller says, "Going from Leicester to Coventry we pass by two Engine Houses which are wrought by fire and throw a great quantity of water out of the pits." At Coventry he notes, "Here's an Antient Custom of Riding Lady Godiva, &c. Every year the Effigie of the man is fixed against the wall of a house, who looked at her while she was riding through the city." From Coventry he went through Banbury, Deddington and Woodstock, and returned to Reading about the middle of August.

The same book contains notes of things to be done, purchases and enquiries to be made on the journey, and various other private and business records, suggestions, and memoranda. Some of these are interesting as showing the varied nature of the enterprises he was engaged in and the activity of his nature; others are curious; all are characteristic and seem to give us a slight glimpse of the personality of this busy and energetic man.

Very early in the book we find the two following notes, which show the true business instinct:—

"At my return advertize all sorts of the haberdashery and cutlery goods that I keep to be sold wholesale as cheap as in the country where made, only paying 2½ per cent commission, and write on door, goods sold by commission from the makers per John Newbery & Co., for ready money only, *and so excuse one's self from trusting.*"

"Get a note in the following manner to secure Mr Collier's debt, viz., let Mr Collier give a promissory note of his hand to Mr Morsham, then Mr Morsham indorse it to Mrs Blackhead, and Mrs Blackhead indorse it to me. *This is better than any joint note, because all the indorsers are liable.*"

Here is another scheme, "let Mr Micklewright print a *Reading Mercury and Advertiser* once a fortnight, and J. Carnan print a *Reading Mercury and Weekly Post* once a fortnight, and by that means save duty of advertisements. Note, let the titles be *The Reading Mercury* and *The Reading Courant.*"

Whether this idea was ever carried out or not does not appear; most likely not. There was a *Reading Journal and Weekly Review*, started in 1741, but it does not appear to have had a long or successful career.

The shop at Reading, the Bible and Crown in the Market Place, the site of the offices of the *Mercury,* must have contained a miscellaneous assortment of goods. He seems to have bought or noted the prices of anything and everything he thought he could sell. Memoranda of cutlery and haberdashery of all sorts, and medicines of various kinds, books, stationery, bought and to buy, occur frequently, and wherever he went his mind appears to have been constantly on his business.

Among other things he records the purchase of
New Small Pica [type], 250 lbs., at 4d.,
Brevier (Old), 331 lbs., at 5d.,
Mr Bowyer's Pica, 300 lbs., at 5d.,
the cost of which may interest the printers of today. In most
of the entries of this kind the prices are in cypher. This one
is given in plain figures.

Several recipes for medicine occur in this little book,
some for private use, such as "for my common cooling
drink;" others evidently are noted that they may be
manufactured on his return home. But perhaps the most
interesting are the literary notes and memoranda of books to
be published, which we think are worth being recorded
here.

Print (Price 6d.)
A collection of curious Mottos from Greek, Latin, French and
English Authors, for the use of Poets and Puppeys, by Lawrence
Likelihood, Esq.;   also,
The Norfolk Dumplins.

To put Mr Walker on Printing an Abridgement of the History
of the World (but not call it an abridgement), and get a patent
for it, to which add the present State of all Nations, from
Salmon;
Likewise,
A Body of Divinity, compiled from Usher Fiddes and
Stackhouse's Body of Divinity.

Write pamphlets from Stackhouse's Body of Divinity, and from
Puffendorff's Law of Nature and Nations, and Salmon's present
State of all Nations.

Put Mr Walker on Printing
The Duty of Man, in all Sizes; also,
Salmon's abridgement of State Tryal,   and
Admiral Norris's Ship the *Victory.*

The following note is probably with a view to self-improvement:—

> To read Blackwall's Sacred Classics, 2 vols. 12mo, and Rollin's Ancient and Modern History and Roman History, with his Arts and Sciences, 8vo.

> Tell Mr Walker to send Mr Rowbottom a set of Mr Whitfield's Sermons, bound and lettered. Publish the Letters and Remarks on them by special authority for the benefit of the poor.

> Publish a copperplate of the view of Yarmouth, with a proper description of its large mouth, great cavities and harbour. The town and citadel cloathed in hoop petticoats, Madam Valmodon.[1]

> Print a plain and rational vindication and explanation of the Liturgy of the Church of England, &c., by J. Clutterbuck, Gent., the 7th edition, printed by E. and R. Nutt, and sold by S. Birt, 1727. Get it revised and corrected by a Clergyman, who shall put his name to it, and print it in longprimer 12mo and English 8vo, and do 2,000 of each, and recommend them to be given away, and give some away yourself stitched, against Christmas.

> Print a treatise on death from Erasmus, Drilingcourt, Sherlock, &c., with prayers &c., proper to be given away at funerals and a companion to the Altar, both to be sold with the Liturgy, to be bound with Common Prayer, or without.

> Print the Alcoran of Mahomet, translated from the Arabick Language by Father La Mo Che, and made English from his Latin manuscript by Robert Nixon, D.D. Do it from the 4th

---

[1] Very shortly after the death of his Queen (Caroline), George II created one of his mistresses, the Baroness Walmoden, Countess of Yarmouth. The date of her creation is March 24, 1740. This has been described as the last instance of the scandalous abuse of the royal prerogative and prostitution of the honours of the State. Doubtless Newbery shared the public indignation against Madam Valmodon, as he calls her, and intended to pillory her in his "Copperplate Views of Yarmouth." — W.

translation, and add notes on the extravagances thereof.

To all well-disposed charitable people, this is to give notice, that this day is published, *for the benefit of the Poor of the Church of England,* a vindication, &c., of the Liturgy, a Companion, &c., to the altar, and a preparatory to death, translated from Erasmus, all for one shilling. This is a proper book for zealous Christians to give their poor neighbours, and it is printed in different sizes to bind with the Common Prayer.

The next entry, like a former one, seems to point to a course of private reading for self-instruction —

Read Blackwall's Rhetorick, Stirling's Rhetorick, Holms's Rhetorick, Brightland's Rhetorick, and Rollin's Rhetorick, and read one trope at a time, and after comparing the books together, enter the examples of them all in one little book, and look for instances in Pope's Homer's Iliad.

The works of the Whole Duty of Man are —
    1. The Whole Duty of Man.
    2. The Gentleman's Calling.
    3. The Ladies Calling.
    4. The Cause of the Decay of Christianity.
    5. The Government of the Tongue.
    6. The Oracle of the Holy Scriptures. Printed at Oxon in the year 1696.

All in the hands of the Rev. Mr Williams at Ashbury, in Cheshire, near Congleton.

Note. — Publish other books as printed by the author of the Whole Duty of Man, and handed from one gentleman to another, and at last given me by a friend and (show the letter with the name torn off). . .

To print a Sermon preached at the wedding of the Lady Eliz. —— by her Ladyship's desire from the following words — Hebrews, chap.13, verse 4:

"Marriage is honourable in all, and the bed undefiled; but whoremongers and adulterers God will judge."

Wrote by her Ladyship, and preached by her order on the day of her nuptials.   J.M.B.D.

Publish Transmigration plainly proved by several theorems — humbly addressed to the Royal Society by the author of Man Wallop. To which is added a Receipt to make a Dessert for the Ladies after drinking Tea from the Calf's Head.

Returning to Reading, Newbery proceeded to carry out vigorously the schemes with which his mind had been busied while travelling up and down the country. The first book that I can find with his imprint is dated Reading, 1740. In 1742, Newbery appears to have been in some way associated with C. Micklewright, whose name appears conjointly with his on several imprints for the next two or three years.[1]

In 1743, John Newbery, with three others, entered into an agreement with John Hooper of Reading, for the better selling and disposing of his "female pills," paying him £100 for the right to vend them for fourteen years. The original document, signed at the Three Tuns, Reading, is still in possession of the family.

Newbery's connection with Benjamin Collins, of Salisbury, who printed the first edition of *The Vicar of Wakefield*, began at about this time, and they continued for several years in business relations. Many of Collins's business records are preserved, and they throw much interesting

---

[1] *The Whole Duty of Man,* referred to above, was produced in association with Micklewright and advertised in the *Reading Mercury* for August 18, 1740. Mrs M.F. Thwaite, in the introduction to her edition of *A Little Pretty Pocket-Book* (Oxford, 1966) says that the other book published by Newbery in 1740 was *Miscellaneous Works. . . for the Amusement of the Fair Sex,* of which there is a copy in the Bodleian Library. It was printed by John Carnan, Newbery's elder stepson, and sold by Newbery at his Reading office. "As yet," adds Mrs Thwaite, "there is no sign of any venture into juvenile publishing." — T.

light on some important literary schemes.[1]

In the year 1744 we find from Newbery's advertisements in the public prints that he has opened a warehouse at the Bible and Crown, near Devereux Court, without Temple Bar, London, with a branch establishment, for the convenience of supplying merchants and captains of ships, country shopkeepers, &c., at the Golden Ball, in Castle Alley, at the Royal Exchange, and we must defer until another chapter such records of his doings in the great metropolis as the scanty materials at command will enable us to give.

---

[1] Collins had dealings with many other publishers besides Newbery, and was associated with several important literary ventures. His account books show among other things that he bought, on June 25, 1761, from Ralph Griffiths a fourth share in *The Monthly Review* for £755. 12s 6d; that *The London Chronicle or Universal Evening Post* was his "own scheme at the setting out;" that he bought of Mr Wm. Strahan in 1757 a sixteenth share in *The Rambler* for £22. 2s 6d, an eighteenth in *Pamela,* April 21, 1763, for £2. 2s; and that he was an equal partner with Wm. Johnson in the venture of publishing Smollett's *Humphrey Clinker,* for which they paid Smollett £210. — W.

CHAPTER II

Removal to St Paul's Churchyard——Dr James's Fever Powder——Dr Johnson——Christopher Smart——The Family Oracle——The Hilliad——Thomas Carnan.

JOHN NEWBERY does not appear to have remained long at "The Bible and Crown, near Devereux Court, without Temple Bar," for the last advertisement from that address appears in *The Penny London Post,* July 24, 1745; and the first from "The Bible and Sun, near the Chapter House, in St Paul's Church-yard" in *The General Evening Post,* August 6, 1745.

Devereux Court was too far west, and the Royal Exchange too far east, for the successful prosecution of his affairs, and accordingly Newbery consolidated his two establishments at St Paul's Churchyard, which was at that time, as now [1885], an important business centre, and long famous as a resort of publishers, all of whom, in the lapse of years, have disappeared from this spot with the exception of the successors of the Newberys.

The house which John Newbery occupied was "over against the north door of the cathedral," and was at the "corner of Pissing (now named Canon) Alley," "near the bar," as it has been variously described. This was, subsequently, when the streets of London were first numbered (according to Cunningham,[1] in 1764-66) known as number 65. It was not until after John Newbery's death in 1767 that Francis Newbery, his nephew, who had been previously issuing books from Paternoster Row, went to 20 Ludgate Street — the corner of St Paul's Churchyard — where the business was continued by his widow, and afterwards by John Harris and his successors.

John Newbery's transactions in London had by this time, according to his son, Francis, "become so multifarious, for he had become a merchant in medicine as well as of books, and had the sole management of the sale of Dr James's celebrated Fever Powder (which was discovered in 1743, though not patented until November, 1746) of which he had purchased half the property,[2] that he became unable to attend to the business at Reading, and therefore gave it up, reserving to himself an annuity from its profits."

He was now settled in St Paul's Churchyard, having apparently by this time found his *métier*, and determined to confine his business to book publishing and medicine vending. He was, says his son, "in the full employment of his talents in writing and publishing books of amusement and instruction for children. The call for them was immense, an edition of many thousands being sometimes exhausted during the Christmas holidays. His friend Dr Samuel

---

[1] P.Cunningham, *Handbook of London* (London, 1850) — T.

[2] The agreement is dated February 23, 1746, and is between Robert James, of St Paul's, Covent Garden, and John Newbery, of St Paul's Churchyard, bookseller, for 21 years to make his pills for the gout, rheumatism, king's evil, scurvy and leprosy, and to sell them to J. Newbery for 8d per box, each box containing 2 pills — 1 pill a dose — and his fever powder at 8d per box, each containing 2 doses. Newbery had the sole sale, and the doctor was to prescribe the same medicines, but under another form, for his private patients, agreeing not to undersell Newbery. The Doctor was to pay Newbery a royalty on the medicines sold abroad. Newbery was not to make them or disclose the secret, but the recipe was to be sealed for the use of his executors. . . — W.

Johnson, who, like other grave characters, could now and then be jocose, had used to say of him, 'Newbery is an extraordinary man, for I know not whether he has read or written most books."

Of the connection between Dr Johnson and Newbery, who probably became acquainted about this period, there is not much to be recorded, though they evidently often met and had business transactions together, and were excellent friends through life. Prior, in his *Life of Goldsmith*[1], gives seven memoranda of money borrowed by Dr Johnson from Mr Newbery. The dates range from 1751 to 1760. In one note, August 24, 1751, Dr Johnson says, "I beg the favour of you to lend me another guinea." In 1759 and 1760, Johnson passed to Newbery his note of hand for £42 and £30: it is presumed for advances on account of *The Idler.* It is not clear whether it was through Dr James that Newbery became acquainted with Dr Johnson or whether it was Dr Johnson who introduced him to James. Both belonged to Lichfield, and they were in their early days intimately associated.

Dr James, according to Francis Newbery, "soon acquired a large practice and became a fashionable physician. He was a profound scholar, an excellent chemist, and an admirable physician. He probably might not have attained the eminence he did had it not been for the fortunate discovery of his fever powder; for at his outset, and for several years afterwards, he was in embarrassed circumstances, and gained a livelihood principally by writing for the booksellers. He always expressed the highest regard for Mr John Newbery, declaring that without his friendship and exertions he should not have been able to establish his medicines. Indeed, after their connection he [James] sold a part of his share in the concern to Mr Benjamin Collins of Salisbury, in order to raise a sum of which he stood in need. Mr Collins having

[1] James Prior, *Life of Oliver Goldsmith* (London, 1837). — T.

some time after repented of his bargain, Mr Newbery paid him back the purchase money with interest, and made the doctor a present of the assignment.

"After such an act of generosity it is no wonder that the happiest understanding should have prevailed, and have continued uninterrupted during life, both with Mr Newbery and with his son.[1]

"In Dr James's time it was not considered derogatory in the profession to sell a nostrum. Sir Hans Sloane, the President of the Royal Society, vended an eye salve, and Dr Mead, the Court Physician, sold a nostrum which it was pretended would cure the bite of a mad dog. In that age every successful man was lampooned or caricatured, very

---

[1] Goldsmith, in a paper on "Quacks Ridiculed" (*Public Ledger*, 1760), brought Newbery to some extent under his lash, for at that time he was advertising at least a dozen patent medicines of the day. And when the old house at the corner of St Paul's Churchyard was, in 1885, pulled down and rebuilt, a panel was discovered over the fireplace in the shop with the inscription 'Newbery's Medicinal Warehouse,' and a list of over thirty different nostrums, among which it is curious to note the following:

Dr James's Powder	Arquebusade Water
Dr Steer's Oil for	Hungary Balsam
Convulsions	Rowley's Herb Snuff
Dr Hooper's Female Pills	English Coffee
Glass's Magnesia	Cephalic Snuff
Henry's Calcined Magnesia	Kennedy's Corn Plaister
Mrs Norton's Mordant Drops	Issue Plaister
Beaume de Vie	Hemet's Dentifrice
Greenough's Lozenges of Tolu	Hemet's Essence
Stomachic Lozenges	Greenough's Tincture
Grant's Drop(?s)	Ormskirk Medicine
Hill's Balsam of Honey	Dr Bateman's Drops
English's Scots Pills	Dr Norris's Pills
Dicey's Scots Pills	Dalby's Carminative Mixture
Cook's Rheumatic Powder	— W.

John Newbery's list of medicines, as advertised in his publications up to the time of his death, was much shorter, so some of the above were obviously added by his successors. — T.

often both, and Dr James did not escape."

Horace Walpole was an enthusiastic votary of James's powder, which he seems to have regarded as a sovereign preventive for almost all diseases. He writes to Sir Horace Mann in October, 1764: "James' powder is my panacea; that is, it always shall be, for, thank God, I am not apt to have occasion for medicines; but I have such faith in these powders that I believe I should take them if the house were on fire."

Dr James dedicated his *Medicinal Dictionary,* a laborious work, which was compiled for the booksellers, to Dr Mead, then a fashionable physician. The dedication was written by Dr Johnson, and in his happiest style. In relation to this, Boswell says:— "Johnson now had an opportunity of obliging his schoolfellow Dr James, of whom he once observed, 'No man brings more mind to his profession.' James published this year [1743] his *Medicinal Dictionary* in three volumes folio. Johnson, as I understood from him, had written, or attested in writing, the proposals for this work; and being very fond of the study of physic, in which James was his master, he furnished some of the articles. He, however, wrote for it the dedication to Dr Mead, which is conceived with great address, to conciliate the patronage of that very eminent man." The poet Christopher Smart testifies to the merits of the fever powder by dedicating to Dr James his *Hymn to the Supreme Being,* on recovery from a dangerous fit of illness.

This association with medicine, and its practitioners, would naturally give a man like Newbery some knowledge of the subject, doubtless to be increased by the study of its literature, which at that period however was often diverting enough by its fanciful foolishness; and it appears by some letters from his brother, who was a small farmer at Waltham St Lawrence, in 1752-3, that he was looked upon, by his family at least, as an oracle upon other matters than books.

The horses and "horned Cattell" in that district were attacked by a distemper, and John was consulted as to what should be done.[1] What his reply was does not appear,but he managed to spare some time to run away from his London business, for his brother writes in January, 1753, "Mr Sharp takes it very ill that you should come twice into the contery and not call upon him, therefore when you comes to Windsor again pray if can come as far as our place, for he says if he had known that you had bein at Windsor he wold have come to have seen you, for he wants very much to see you. — From your affect. Brother, ROBERT NEWBERY."

It was about this period, 1750-52, that Newbery became acquainted with Christopher Smart, who in 1753 married Miss Anna Maria Carnan, one of the daughters, by her first husband, of Mrs Newbery. He had been introduced to this family by Dr Burney, the celebrated author of the *History of Music,* who set to music several of Smart's songs.

The Rev. C. Hunter, in the life of Smart which is prefixed to the *Poems,*[2] says that Newbery and Smart, who were engaged together in some general scheme of authorship, were the chief, if not the only, contributors to *The Midwife, or the Old Woman's Magazine,* a small periodical pamphlet, which was published in threepenny numbers, and afterwards collected into three volumes, 12mo. It consists of small pieces in prose and verse, mostly of the humorous kind, and generally in a style of humour which, at the present time, would be reckoned somewhat coarse.

Smart was a master of the art of puffing, and in him no

---

[1] This distemper among the cattle was very widespread at the time, and there are several letters extant to Newbery from all parts of the country with reference to the use of Dr James's Fever Powder made up in larger doses for the animals. — W.

[2] *The Poems of the late Christopher Smart, M.A., &c*.: Reading. Printed and sold by Smart & Cowslade: and sold by F. Power & Co., No. 65, St Paul's Churchyard, London, MDCCXCI. — W.

doubt Newbery, who was, if possible, a greater adept in the practice, found a very useful ally. The publication of Smart's poems by him, in 1752, elicited an adverse criticism in the *Monthly Review,* which Smart supposed was by Dr (afterwards, as he styled himself, Sir) John Hill. For this and other offences, Smart took his revenge in *The Hilliad.*[1]

During Smart's unfortunate mental attacks, he was constantly befriended by Newbery; but "in the course of a few years," says the Rev. C. Hunter, "Smart was confined for debt in the King's Bench prison, the rules[2] of which he afterwards obtained by the kindness of his brother-in-law, Mr Thomas Carnan.

"He [Smart] died after a short illness on May 18, 1770[3], of a disorder in his liver, leaving behind him two daughters, who, with his widow, are settled at Reading in Berkshire, and by their prudent management of a business, transferred to them by the late Mr John Newbery, are in good circumstances."

This Thomas Carnan, who was one of Newbery's stepsons, appears to have come with him to London, and to have been very intimately associated with him in his business, chiefly in the retailing department and attending to the shop generally. Later on, several books bore his imprint: probably the earliest was *The Midwife* (1751), and Newbery's reason for this arrangement may have been that he did not wish his name, which was becoming widely known as a publisher of

---

[1] Hill, who claimed the title Sir as a member of a Swedish order, was an apothecary who became a medical doctor, botanist and miscellaneous writer. His satirical and scurrilous writings (says the *Dictionary of National Biography*) frequently involved him in squabbles; Johnson said he was "an ingenious man but had no veracity." — T.

[2] Obtaining the rules: getting permission to live in a defined area outside the prison walls. — T.

[3] *DNB* says May 21, 1771. — T.

books for children, to be associated with such a production. Newbery is. however, alluded to more than once both in this book and in *The Nonpareil.*

CHAPTER III

First employment of Goldsmith—Odd medicines—Dr Johnson and *The Idler*—Smollett and *The British Magazine*—The *Public Ledger*—Griffith Jones—Residence at Canonbury Tower—Newbery's relations with Goldsmith—The Jelly Bag Society—A printing patent—Last illness and death.

WE have now arrived at the most important and active period of John Newbery's career. Busily as he was engaged during the preceding years, the last eleven of his life, from 1757 to 1767, appear to have been even more fully occupied. His medicine business had grown to large dimensions; his publishing ventures had become more numerous and more important; and his literary associations were more widely extended. Larger numbers of his famous little books for children were issued during this period, and it would be in about 1757 or 1758 that he first became associated with Goldsmith, who from almost his earliest connection with Newbery seems to have been constantly supplied with small advances of money by him, which, as Forster says in his *Life of Goldsmith*, "became a hopeless entanglement." The *Literary Magazine* was one of Newbery's ventures, and Prior [in his *Life of Goldsmith* previously cited] thinks that Goldsmith's first work for Newbery was an article in that magazine for January, 1758.

To turn for a moment from books to medicine. We find

that in 1757 Newbery entered into an agreement with James Grosett of Charterhouse Square for making and selling the Lisbon or German Doctor's Diet-Drink, the Unguent de Cao, and the Angola Ptisane. These recipes are curious and one or two revolting. The basis for the Unguent is as follows:—"Get a good fat young dog alive, and when you are prepared with two gallons of water, or as much as is necessary to cover him, knock him on the head and throw him into it." Other ingredients, almost as extraordinary, were to be added, and the whole boiled and strained according to directions.

In 1758, taking advantage of that rage for intelligence which the successes of the war had excited in even the lower orders of the people, Newbery projected a weekly newspaper called *The Universal Chronicle or Weekly Gazette*, the first number of which appeared on April 15, and it continued to be issued for the next two years. Dr Johnson's celebrated *Idler* was first printed in this journal. He was allowed a share, and as the size of the paper rendered it susceptible of more matter than the occurrences during the intervals of its publication would supply, it was part of the scheme that it should contain a short essay on such subjects of morality or wit and humour as in former instances had been found to engage the attention of the public. Mr John Payne, according to Chalmers,[1] was associated with Newbery in the enterprise, and the share in the profits was Johnson's inducement to furnishing the essays. "Most of them," says Chalmers, "were written in haste in various places where he happened to be on the eve of publication, and with very little preparation. A few of them exhibit the train of thought which prevails in the *Rambler;* but in general they have a vivacity and exhibit a species of

---

[1] Alexander Chalmers (1759-1834), biographer, miscellaneous writer, and editor of *The British Essayists* (1802). — T.

grace and humour in which Johnson excelled. When the *Universal Chronicle* was discontinued, these papers were collected into two small volumes, which he corrected for the press, making a few alterations and omitting one whole paper, which has since been restored."

"Now, week by week," says Mr Forster in his life of Goldsmith, "in a paper of Mr John Newbery's, Johnson sent forth the *Idler*. What he was, and what with a serious earnestness, be it wrong or right, he had come into the world to say and do, were at last becoming evident to all. Colleges were glad to have him visit them, and a small enthusiastic circle was gradually forming around him. The Reynoldses, Bennet Langtons and Topham Beauclercs had thus early given their allegiance, and Arthur Murphy was full of wonder at his submitting to contradiction, when they dined together this last Christmas day with young Mr Burke at Wimpole Street. But not more known or conspicuous was the consideration thus exacted than the poverty which still waited on it and claimed its share. So might literature avenge herself, in this penniless champion, for the disgrace of the money bags of Walpole and Pelham. 'I have several times called on Johnson,' wrote Grainger to Percy,[1] 'to pay him part of your subscription' (for his edition of Shakespeare.) 'I say part, because he never thinks of working if he has a couple of guineas in his pocket.' And again, a month later: 'As to his Shakespeare, *movet, sed non promovet.* I shall feed him occasionally with guineas.' It was thus the good Mr Newbery found it best to feed him too. For, in his worst distress, it was still but of literature Mr Johnson begged or borrowed: to her he was indebted for his poverty, and to her only would he owe his independence."

Speaking of the want of news to fill the *Universal*

---

[1] James Grainger (1721?-66), physician and poet; Thomas Percy (1729-1811), editor of the *Reliques of Ancient English Poetry.* — T.

Chronicle, Chalmers says in his *Life of Smollett*, "It is a curious particular in the history of political intelligence. Those who now print weekly papers find it not only difficult but impossible to contain half of the articles which have entertained other readers during the intervals of publication and which, from the common impulse of domestic or public curiosity, their readers think they have a right to expect. Let it be remembered, however, that to the editor of a newspaper the *Parliamentary Proceedings* were then forbidden fruit.

"During the latter months of 1759, whilst Smollett was in the King's Bench Prison, Newbery was planning a sixpenny monthly magazine, to be started with the coming year, which was called *The British Magazine, or Monthly Repository for Gentlemen and Ladies, by T. Smollett, M.D., and others*. He [Newbery] was an honest fellow of some sense and ability, and his feelings with regard to literary men were as humane as those of his neighbour Griffiths were the reverse. He had lately, in a manner, rescued Goldsmith from the bondage of the Griffiths' warehouse garret, and he had secured the services of the ingenious but as yet unknown person for the intended new magazine. As an editor for that publication, Newbery engaged the imprisoned Smollett, and with his name on the title, and under protection of a royal patent, which was obtained through the interest which Smollett had established with Mr Pitt by the late dedication, it made its first appearance before the public in 1760."

Mr Forster, in his life of Goldsmith, thus describes the beginning of this venture:— "But Dr Smollett and Mr Newbery have been waiting for us all this while, and neither of them belonged to that leisurely class which can very well afford to wait. The Doctor was always full of energy and movement; and who remembers not the philanthropic bookseller in *The Vicar of Wakefield*, the good-natured man with the red pimpled face, who was no sooner alighted than he was in haste to be gone, 'for he was ever on business of the utmost importance, and he was at that time actually compiling materials for the history of Mr Thomas Trip'? But not on Mr Thomas Trip's affairs had the child-loving publisher now ventured up breakneck stairs; and upon other than the old Critical business was the author of *Peregrine Pickle* a visitor in Green Arbour Court. Both had new and important schemes in hand, and with both it was an object to secure the alliance and services of Goldsmith. Smollett had, at all times, not a little of the Pickle in him, and Newbery much of the Mr Trip; but there was a genial goodheartedness in both which makes it natural and pleasant to have to single out these two men as the first active friends and patrons of the author of the unsuccessful *Bee.*"

Newbery's next work of importance was the issue of the *Public Ledger,* of which Forster gives the following account:— "War is the time for newspapers. The inventive head which planned the *Universal Chronicle,* with the good taste that enlisted Johnson in its service, now made a bolder effort in the same direction, and the first number of the *Public Ledger* was published on January 12, 1760. Nothing less than a daily newspaper had the busy publisher of children's books projected. But a daily newspaper was not an appalling speculation then. Not then, morning after morning, did it throw its eyes of Argus over all the world. No universal command was needed for it then, over sources of foreign intelligence potent to dispose and to control the money transactions of rival hemispheres. The *Public Ledger* called itself simply a daily register of commerce and intelligence, and fell short of even such modest pretensions. 'We are unwilling,' said the Editor in its first number, 'to raise expectations which we may perhaps find ourselves unable to satisfy; and therefore they have no mention of criticism or literature, which yet we do not professionally exclude; nor shall we reject any political essays which are apparently calculated for the public good.' Discreetly avoiding all undue expectations, there quietly came forth into the world, from Mr Bristow's office, next the great toy-shop in St Paul's Churchyard, the first number of the *Public Ledger.* It was circulated gratis, with the announcement that all future numbers would be sold for twopence-halfpenny each.

"The first four numbers were enlightened by Probus in politics and Sir Simeon Swift in literature, the one defending the war,[1] the other commencing the *Ranger*, and both very mildly justifying the modest editorial announcements. The fifth number was not so commonplace. It had a letter vindicating with manly assertion the character and courage of the then horribly unpopular French, and humorously condemning the national English habit of abusing rival nations, which implied a larger spirit as it showed a livelier pen.

"The same hand again appeared in the next number but one; and the correspondent of Green Arbour Court [i.e. Goldsmith] became entitled to receive two guineas from Mr Newbery for his first week's contribution to the *Public Ledger.* His arrangement was to write twice in the week and to be paid a guinea for each article.

"In these early numbers of the *Public Ledger,* Goldsmith wrote the Chinese Letters. At the close of 1760," continues Forster, "ninety-eight of the letters had been published; within the next few months, at less regular intervals, the series was brought to completion; and in the following year the whole were republished by Mr Newbery 'for the Author,' in two duodecimo volumes, but without any author's name, as *The Citizen of the World; or, Letters from a Chinese*

---

[1] The Seven Years War (1756-63), fought by the major European powers over European and colonial territories and commercial rivalries. Britain took the side of Prussia and Hanover against France, Austria, Russia, Poland and Sweden. French and British fought in North America, and in the end, the Treaty of Paris gave Canada to Britain. — T.

Philosopher in London to his friend in the East."

The *Public Ledger* was then printed at the Register Office, and bore the name of W. Bristow, who also appears as the publisher of the pamphlet on *The Cock Lane Ghost,* for which Newbery paid Goldsmith £3. 3s. The first collected edition of the Chinese Letters also bore Bristow's name in the imprint; and at the end of *Goody Two-Shoes* there is "a letter from the printer, which he desires may be inserted," signed W.B., which may have been this same Bristow.

That Bristow was in any way concerned in the venture, beyond being the printer, does not appear probable. But in an "Account of Copies, their Cost and Value, 1764," kept by Benjamin Collins of Salisbury, I find the following entry:— "The *Public Ledger or Daily Register,* a daily newspaper published in London, — my own scheme, in which I have one share and an half. . . first expense was £45," which seems to show that the credit for the idea does not belong to Newbery, as has all along been supposed.[1]

The original editor of the *Public Ledger* is said by some to have been Kelly the dramatist; others say that Griffith Jones held the post. Mr Griffith Jones was, it is certain, very intimately associated with Newbery in his ventures, though it is impossible now to trace his work. In Nichols's *Literary Anecdotes*[2] the following account of him is given:—

"Griffith Jones was born in 1722, and served his apprenticeship with Mr Bowyer [William Bowyer, printer.] Of

---

[1] Here Welsh reproduces in a footnote an agreement for farming out the paper, made six years after Newbery's death. The point of interest is that it bears the signatures of three 'Proprietors': Charles Waller, Hanley Crowden, and 'Thomas Carnan, for Mrs Mary Newbery', i.e. Newbery's stepson, signing on behalf of his mother, who was Newbery's widow. That Newbery had a major involvement in the *Public Ledger* is clear. — T.

[2] John Nichols, printer and miscellaneous writer (1745-1826), published his *Literary Anecdotes of the Eighteenth Century* in nine volumes in 1812-15. — T.

this ingenious man [Jones] slighter notice has been taken by the biographers of the time than his virtues and talents certainly merited. He was many years editor of the *London Chronicle*, the *Daily Advertiser*, and the *Public Ledger*. In the *Literary Magazine* with Johnson, and in the *British Magazine* with Smollett and Goldsmith, his anonymous labours were also associated.

"The native goodness of his heart endeared him to a numerous and respectable literary acquaintance, among whom he reckoned the philanthropic Mr John Newbery, Mr Woty the ingenious poet,[1] Dr Oliver Goldsmith, and the pious and learned Dr S. Johnson, to the latter of whom he was for several years a near neighbour in Bolt Court, Fleet Street. His modesty shrank from public attention, but his labours were frequently directed to the improvement of the younger and more untutored classes of mankind. His translations from the French were very numerous, but as he rarely, if ever, put his name to the productions of his pen, they cannot now be traced. One publication entitled *Great Events from Little Causes* was his composition, and it met with a rapid and extensive sale.

"It is not perhaps generally known that to Mr Griffith Jones and a brother of his, Mr Giles Jones, in conjunction with Mr John Newbery, the publick are indebted for the origin of those numerous and popular little books for the amusement and instruction of children, which have been ever since received with universal approbation. The Lilliputian histories of *Goody Two Shoes, Giles Gingerbread, Tommy Trip* &c. &c., are remarkable proofs of the benevolent minds of the projectors of this plan of instruction, and respectable instances of the accommodation

---

[1] The ingenious William Woty (1731?-1790) is described in the *Dictionary of National Biography* as a "versifier." He was a Grub Street writer who published a collection of "poetical essays, moral and comic" called *The Shrubs of Parnassus.* — T.

of superior talents to the feeble intellects of infantine felicity. Mr Jones died September 12, 1786."[1]

It was during this period of his life (1760-67) that John Newbery had, according to his son Francis, "apartments at Canonbury House, Islington, and for some time Dr Goldsmith resided also in the upper story, the situation so commonly devoted to poets. Dr Goldsmith was particularly attentive to John Newbery's son, Francis, and often read to him passages from the works he had in hand, particularly some favourite portions of *The Traveller,* and stanzas from his beautiful tale of *The Hermit,*[2] introduced into *The Vicar of Wakefield.* These communications were probably intended, like Molière's to his old woman, as an experiment to discover whether his verses were natural and affecting to an unsophisticated mind. Our young man was delighted, and the public judgment has since sufficiently confirmed his taste."

Canonbury House is generally supposed to have been originally built in 1362, and Stow[3] says that it was rebuilt by William Bolton, the last Prior of St Bartholomew's, Smithfield, and was the seat of "the rich" Sir John Spencer, Lord Mayor in 1593, and Lord Keeper Coventry. In it have lodged, besides Newbery, Goldsmith, Christopher Smart, Samuel Humphreys, poet; Ephraim Chambers, cyclopaedist, who died here in 1740; Onslow, the speaker; Woodfall, who printed *Junius*; and Dr John Hill died here. There are many allusions to Canonbury Tower in the writings of the period, and the following lines have often been quoted:—

---

[1] Nichols took this account from Stephen Jones's *New Biographical Dictionary,* published some years earlier. On the authorship of *Goody Two-Shoes* and other titles, see my opening essay. — T.

[2] Goldsmith himself seems never to have given it this title. In *The Vicar of Wakefield* it is simply a ballad. — W.

[3] John Stow (c.1525-1605), antiquary. — T.

See on the distant slope, majestic shews
Old Canonbury's tow'r, an antient pile,
To various fates assign'd, and where by turns,
Meanness and grandeur have alternate reign'd.
Thither, in later days, hath *genius* fled,
From yonder city, to respire and die.
There the sweet bard of Auburn[1] sat and turn'd
The plaintive moanings of his village dirge;
There learned Chambers treasur'd lore for *men,*
And Newbery there his A, B, Cs for *babes.*

— FOX.

The *Pasquinade,* a scurrilous poem by William Kendrick, aimed at Dr Hill, has the couplet:—

With Cyder muddled or inspired with Bub,[2]
In Newb'ry's Garret or in Henley's[3] Tub.

In an article in *The Midwife,* one of Newbery's publications, No.4, vol. ii., entitled *A Remarkable Prediction of an Author, who shall write an history of England in the year 1931,* we find the following:—

And this is farther prov'd and confirm'd by Mr Caxall, the antiquarian, who hath now by him a walking Staff dug out of the ruins of Canbury House, near Islington, which is four foot long, and on it are engraved the letters NEWBERY, probably the Same Newbery who wrote the heroic poem entitled *The Benefit of eating Beef* (of which

---

[1] Goldsmith, who gave this name to his Deserted Village. — T.

[2] Bub, a strong malt liquor which was much drunk at that time, but not indulged in except by the vulgar. — W.

[3] "Orator Henley," as he was called. He set up an oratory in Newport Market, where he lectured in such a vulgar and abusive style that he was stopped by the authorities. — W.

CANONBURY TOWER ABOUT 1800.

there now remain some fragments with the commentary of one Smart), a Sort of Food much in repute in those days, though now not digestable by our puny Stomacks; and if the Same, he was not a very tall man, if we may believe the biographer who wrote his life, which is prefixed to the poem.[1]

The tower of Canonbury House still exists (1885), but it is in a sadly dilapidated state. Although the exterior looks substantial enough, and the splendid carved wood panelling of some of the rooms is intact, all of them are deserted and many are decaying, and unless it is speedily put into a proper state of repair it will rapidly tumble to pieces. So interesting a building, both on account of its historic and its literary associations, should surely be preserved, and something done to mark the sense of veneration which all lovers of English literature and history must naturally have for such a spot.[2]

The precise period during which Goldsmith lived in Canonbury Tower, or the exact spot of the lodging which he occupied near thereto, cannot be ascertained. It was certainly somewhere about this time; and of the relations between Newbery and Goldsmith during their residence at Islington and subsequently, Forster gives the following account:—

"That he had come here with designs of labour, more constant and unremitting than ever, new and closer arrangements with Newbery would appear to indicate. The publisher made himself, with certain prudent limitations, Mrs Fleming's paymaster; board and lodging were to be charged £50 a year" — the reader has to keep in mind that

---

[1] The poem and the biography alike apparently only existed in this facetious writer's imagination. — W.

[2] It was restored in 1907. — T.

this would be now nearly double that amount[1] — and, when the state of their accounts permitted it, to be paid each quarter by Mr Newbery, the publisher taking credit for these payments in his literary settlements with Goldsmith. The first quarterly payment had become due on March 24, 1763, and on that day the landlady's claim of £12. 10s., made up to £14 by "incidental expenses," was discharged by Newbery. It stands as one item in an account of his cash advances for the first nine months of 1763, which characteristically exhibits the relations of book-writer and bookseller. Mrs Fleming's bills recur at their stated intervals, and on September 8 there is a payment of £15 to William Filby the tailor. The highest advance in money is one (which is not repeated) of three guineas; the rest vary, with intervals of a week or so between each, from two guineas to one guinea and half a guinea. The whole amount, from January to October, 1763, is little more than £96, upwards of £60 of which Goldsmith had meanwhile satisfied by copy of different kinds, when on settlement day he gave his note for the balance. [See next page.]

The subjoined is from a copy in Goldsmith's own handwriting——

Brookes' *History*, £11.11s; preface to *Universal History*, £3.3s; preface to *Rhetoric*, £2.2s; preface to *Chronicle*, £1.1s; *History of England*, £21; *The Life of Christ*, £10.10s; *The Life* (sic) *of the Fathers*, £10.10s; *Critical* and *Monthly*, £3.3s; Total, £63.

Received, Oct. 11, 1763 . . . Oliver Goldsmith.

Mr Forster gives all the accounts between Mrs Fleming and Goldsmith which have been preserved, and one of

---

[1] Forster was writing in the 1840s. The multiplier now (1990s) would be something like 60, so Goldsmith's bed and board were costing the equivalent of about £3,000 ($4,500 in early 1994) a year, or roughly £60 ($90) a week, which sounds like good value. — T.

Doctor Goldsmith, debtor to John Newbery

					£	s	d
1761, Oct.	14.	1 set of the *Idler*,	.	.	£0	5	0
1762, Nov.	9.	To cash,	.	.	10	10	0
Dec.	22.	To ditto,	.	.	3	3	0
	29.	To ditto,	.	.	1	1	0
1763, Jan.	22.	To ditto,	.	.	1	1	0
	25.	To ditto,	.	.	1	1	0
Feb.	14.	To ditto,	.	.	1	1	0
March	11.	To ditto,	.	.	2	2	0
	22.	To ditto,	.	.	1	1	0
	24.	To cash paid Mrs Fleming,	.		14	0	0
	30.	To cash,	.	.	0	10	6
May	4.	To cash,	.	.	2	2	0
May	21.	To ditto,	.	.	3	3	0
June	3.	To cash paid Mrs Fleming,	.		14	11	0
June	25.	To cash,	.	.	2	2	0
July	1.	To ditto,	.	.	2	2	0
	20.	To cash paid Mrs Fleming,	.		14	14	0
Sept.	2.	To cash,	.	.	1	1	0
Sept.	8.	To do., paid your draft to Wm. Filby,	.	.	15	2	0
	10.	To cash,	.	.	0	10	6
	19.	To do.,	.	.	1	1	0
	24.	To do.,	.	.	2	2	0
Oct.	8.	To do.,	.	.	2	2	0
	10.	To cash paid your bill to Mrs Fleming,	.	.	14	13	6
					£111	1	6
		By copy of different kinds,	.		63	0	0
Oct.	11.	By note of hand rec'd and delivered up the vouchers,	.	.	£48	1	6

Account rendered ...

them contains the entry "1764, to the rent of the room from December 25 to March 29, £1. 17s 6d.", but whether this was a room in Canonbury Tower, or the lodging which Goldsmith is said to have taken in order to be near Newbery, is by no means clear. It is certain, however, that Newbery paid the accounts of Mrs Fleming, and it seems to me to be not unlikely that Mrs Fleming was the landlady or caretaker of Canonbury House, especially as Francis Newbery tells us that Goldsmith read portions of *The Vicar of Wakefield* to him while he was residing in the upper storey.

In 1766 *The Vicar of Wakefield* was published by Francis Newbery [the nephew] at the Crown, in Paternoster Row. There are probably few points of literary history of the last century more obscure and involved than the story of the writing, and sale of the copyright, of this book. Various and conflicting are the accounts which have been given of it, all of which — though they may have some common basis of truth — are much interlarded with conjecture. The story upon which most of them appear to have been founded is that which Boswell represents Johnson as telling. "I received one morning," says Johnson, "a message from poor Goldsmith that he was in great distress, and, as it was not in his power to come to me, begging that I would come to him as soon as possible. I sent him a guinea, and promised to come to him directly. I accordingly went as soon as I was dressed, and found that his landlady had arrested him for his rent, at which he was in a violent passion. I perceived that he had already changed my guinea, and had a bottle of Madeira and a glass before him. I put the cork into the bottle, desired he would be calm, and began to talk to him of the means by which he might be extricated. He then told me he had a novel ready for the press, which he produced to me. I looked into it, and saw its merit; told the landlady I should soon return; and, having gone to a bookseller, sold it for sixty pounds. I brought Goldsmith the money, and he discharged his rent, not without rating his landlady in a high tone for having used him so ill."

Upon this, Mr Forster, in his *Life of Goldsmith,* raises a whole fabric of ingenious speculation. He says: "Nor does this rating seem altogether undeserved, since there are certainly considerable grounds for suspecting that Mrs Fleming was the landlady. The attempt to clear her seems to me to fail in many essential points. Tracing the previous incidents minutely, it is almost impossible to disconnect her from this consummation of them, with which, at the same time, every trace of Goldsmith's residence in her house is brought to a close. As for the incident itself, it has nothing startling for the reader who is familiar with what has gone before it. It is the old story of distress, with the addition of a right to resent it which poor Goldsmith had not felt till now, and in the violent passion, the tone of indignant reproach, and the bottle of Madeira, one may see that recent gleams of success and of worldly consideration have not strengthened the old habits of endurance. The arrest is plainly connected with Newbery's reluctance to make further advances. Of all Mrs Fleming's accounts found among his papers, the only one unsettled is that for the summer months preceding the arrest;[1] nor can I even resist

---

[1] A fourth version, that of Sir John Hawkins, quoted by Mr Mitford in his *Life,* and strongly smacking of the knight's usual vein, appears to me to point to Islington as the locality of the arrest, though it does not directly confirm that suggestion. "Of the booksellers whom he styled his friends, Mr Newbery was one. This person had apartments in Canonbury House, where Goldsmith often lay concealed from his creditors. Under a pressing necessity, he there wrote his *Vicar of Wakefield,* and for it received of Newbery £40." It does not detract from the value of this evidence, such as it is, that Sir John gives afterwards his own blundering account of the attempted arrest and Johnson's relief, in apparent ignorance that the piece of writing was *The Vicar of Wakefield.* (Forster.) — W.

altogether the suspicion, considering the intimacy between the families of the Newberys and the Flemings which Newbery's bequests in his will show to have existed,[1] that the publisher himself, for an obvious convenience of his own, may have suggested, or at least sanctioned, the harsh proceeding. The MS of the novel (of which more hereafter) seems by both statements, in which the discrepancies are not so great but that Johnson himself may be held accountable for them, to have been produced reluctantly as a last resource; and it is possible, as Mrs Thrale intimates, that it was still regarded as 'unfinished,' but if strong adverse reasons had not existed, Johnson would surely have carried it to Newbery. He did not do this. He went with it to Francis Newbery, the nephew."

But there is no evidence in any existing papers that we can find to show [that] the manuscript of the novel was sold either to Mr John Newbery the elder or to Francis his nephew; nor is there anything to show the date at which the incident which Johnson represents to have taken place occurred, if, indeed, it ever took place at all.

Mr Forster, in referring to the announcement of the forthcoming *Vicar of Wakefield* in 1766, says, "This was the manuscript sold to Newbery's nephew fifteen months before, and it seems impossible satisfactorily to account for the bookseller's delay." Mr Forster would probably be surprised to hear, if he were within reach of mortal voices, that the manuscript of *The Vicar of Wakefield* was sold by Dr Goldsmith no less than four years before its publication, and this simple fact must render many of his most interesting and brilliant descriptive passages of this period of Goldsmith's history little better than worthless.

According to Francis Newbery [son], in the passage from

---

[1] Newbery left fifty guineas each to Mrs Elizabeth Fleming and Mr Thomas Fleming. — T.

his autobiography quoted *ante,* the book may have been written at any time between 1760 and 1766. Indeed, some of Goldsmith's biographers have said that it was written partly at Wine Office Court, where we know he lived before he went to Islington, and partly at Canonbury Tower. These statements so far confirm Francis Newbery's recollections. But another record exists in the account books kept by Benjamin Collins of Salisbury, and if in some ways these accounts make the whole story more perplexing than ever, in others they are useful as shedding a ray of light and truth upon the matter. In a book marked "Account of copies, their cost and value, 1764," I find the following entry:— *"Vicar of Wakefield,* 2 vols. 12mo., ⅓rd. B. Collins, Salisbury, bought of Dr Goldsmith, the author, October 28, 1762, £21." This conclusively shows that the book was finished in 1762, unless Goldsmith had sold it before it was written, a supposition which would entirely upset Johnson's picturesque story about the bottle of Madeira and the irate landlady. Whatever poor "Goldy's" pecuniary difficulties may have been, we cannot imagine that he was guilty of such an act as that of selling his manuscript twice over, which, however, is not entirely unknown in the present day.

Why the book was kept for four years in manuscript after it was sold must still remain a mystery. I am strongly inclined to believe, however, that it was, as has been suggested, in consequence of business arrangements between John Newbery and his nephew Francis. The setting up of Francis at the Crown in Paternoster Row was doubtless one of Newbery's many ingenious business experiments. A fresh outlet for a "new line of books", and which Goldsmith at this very time was labouring at would be a scheme which would very naturally suggest itself to a publisher who had embarked upon so many and so various enterprises as those to which John Newbery put his hand.

On this point Mr Forster speculates thus: "The elder

Newbery may have interposed some claim to a property in the novel, and objected to its appearance simultaneously with *The Traveller* [the poem from which Goldsmith read passages to Francis the son.] He often took part in this way in his nephew's affairs; and thus, for a translation of a French book on philosophy, which the nephew published after the *Vicar*, and which Goldsmith at this very time was labouring at, we find, from the summer account handed in by the elder Newbery, that the latter had himself provided the payment."

All the writers who have spoken of *The Vicar of Wakefield* have jumped to the conclusion that it brought a golden harvest to its publishers, and they have not failed to reproach honest John Newbery for his illiberality in dealing with Oliver Goldsmith in respect of this book. It would have been singular indeed if Newbery, who appears to have paid Goldsmith for every item of work he did for him with no ungenerous hand, had made an exception in the case of this book. The first three editions, as information drawn from an account book of Collins, marked "Publishing book, account of books printed and shares therein, No. 3, 1770 to 1785," clearly shows, resulted in a loss, and the fourth, which was not issued until eight years after the first, started with a balance against it of £2. 16s. 6d., and it was not until that fourth edition had been sold that the balance came out on the right side.

By this time John Newbery was dead, his business was in the hands of his successors, and, in the face of these facts, it cannot be held that Newbery did any but the right thing by Goldsmith in the matter of *The Vicar of Wakefield*. But, even at this time, so little faith had the proprietors — or one of them, at least — in its future success that he, as appears by an item in the account books in his own handwriting, parted with his third share in it, for which he paid £21, for five guineas.

"The literary engagements of Doctor Oliver Goldsmith were meanwhile going on with Newbery [says Forster]; and towards the close of the year [1766?] he appears to have completed a compilation of a kind somewhat novel to him, induced in all probability by his concurrent professional attempts. It was *A Survey of Experimental Philosophy, considered in its present state of improvement;* and Newbery paid him sixty guineas for it.[1]

"The utmost Goldsmith received in the year 1767 from the elder Newbery," Mr Forster further tells us, "would seem to be about £10 for a compilation on a historical subject, *The British Empire.* The concurrent advance of another £10 on his promissory note, though side by side with the ominous shadow of the yet unpaid note of four years preceding, shows their friendly relations subsisting still.

"But the present illness of the publisher, from which he never recovered, had for some months interrupted the

---

[1] I give the memorandum of books lent to Goldsmith for the purpose of this compilation. 'Sent to Dr Goldsmith, Sept 11, 1765, from Canbury (Canonbury) House the copy of the *Philosophy* to be revised, with the Abbé Nollet's Philosophy, and to have an account added of Hale's Ventilator; together with the following Books:— 1. Pemberton's Newton, quarto. 2. Two pamphlets of Mr Franklin's on Electricity. 3. 1 of Ferguson's Astronomy, quarto. 4. D'Alembert's *Treatise of Fluids*, quarto. 5. Martin's Philosophy, 3 vols. 6. Ferguson's Lectures, do. 7. Helsham's, do. 8. Kiel's Introduction, do. 9. Keil's Astronomy, do. 10. *Nature Displayed*, 7 vols. 12mo. [No. 11 missing.] 12. Nollet's *Philosophy*, 3 vols. 12mo.' (Nollet is called Nola and Noletus, Ferguson figures as Fergason and Fergeson, and D'Alembert is transformed into Darlembert, in worthy Mr Newbery's orthography.) (Forster.) — W.

Johnson's expression of doubt as to whether Newbery had read or written more books is ambiguous:— was he commenting on the extent of Newbery's writings or the limitations of his reading, or did he perhaps mean that Newbery had both written and read a great deal? Lists of books lent to Goldsmith suggest that he had a substantial library, though there is of course no certainty that he had read the books he owned. — T.

ordinary course of his business, and its management was gradually devolving on his nephew.[1]

"With the present year ended [Goldsmith's] exclusive reliance on the booksellers, and, as though to mark it more emphatically, his old friend Newbery died;"[2] and Francis Newbery [the son] says that at this time Goldsmith owed him upwards of £200.

I have been content to let Mr Forster tell the story of Newbery's relations with Goldsmith, as I am without materials for reconstructing it from the Newbery side. This account has led us a little out of the chronological order of the events of Newbery's life, of which we now resume the thread. . .

About the year 1762 Newbery contemplated a Child's Grammar, and he offered the task of compiling it, for ten guineas, to one Peter Annet, who had made himself notorious by a crusade against the Bible, for which he had stood twice in the pillory. Goldsmith and Newbery went to visit Annet, who at once agreed to do the work and to write a dedication and append his name. "But Mr Annet," says Newbery in his grave manner, "would putting your name

---

[1] It seems unlikely that the management of Newbery's business was "gradually devolving on his nephew." Francis the nephew had already branched out on his own. Francis the son was at university; most probably Thomas Carnan held the fort. — T.

[2] To the last poor Goldsmith's necessities followed him. At the back of a letter addressed to Newbery, dated March 28, 1767, in which the writer deplores his worthy publisher's illness, and prays to have his heart rejoiced by the re-establishment of his health, I find sundry pencil marks in Newbery's handwriting, which are probably our last remaining traces of his farewell visit to his favourite Society of Arts, of the jokes he heard there, of the good offices he did there, of the mistakes for which half-learned members got laughed at by the learned there. "You can't lay an egg but you must cackle. *Lent Dr Goldsmith for his instrument, 10s 6d.* Combing the horse's tail. Mr Hely's mistaking Tully's Latin for bad Latin." (Forster.) — W.

to it, do you think, increase the value of your book?" A. Why not, sir? N. Consider a bit, Mr Annet. A. Well, sir, I do: what then? N. Why then, sir, you must recollect that you have been pilloried, and that can be no recommendation to any man's book. A. I grant that I have been pilloried, but I am not the first man that has had this accident; besides, sir, the public very often support a man the more for those unavoidable misfortunes. N. Unavoidable, Mr Annet! why, sir, you brought it on yourself by writing against the established religion of your country, and let me tell you, Mr Annet, a man who is supposed to have forfeited his ears on such an account stands but a poor candidate for public favour. A. Well, well, Mr Newbery, it does not signify talking; you either put my name to it, or by G— you publish no book of mine![1]

In the month of June 1762, John Newbery accompanied Francis, his son, to Oxford, where he was afterwards entered at Trinity College. Of this trip, Francis in his autobiography gives the following account: "At the Angel Inn they had apartments. While there, Mr Warton[2] and two

---

[1] Peter Annet (1693-1769) was a noted deist who published in 1761 nine numbers of a paper called the *Free Enquirer,* attacking Old Testament history. He was convicted of blasphemous libel, on the ground that he had ridiculed the Holy Scriptures and tried to "propagate irreligious and diabolical opinions in the minds of his Majesty's subjects and to shake the foundations of the Christian religion and the civil and ecclesiastical government." He was sentenced to a month's imprisonment in Newgate, to stand twice in the pillory, then to have a year's hard labour in Bridewell, and to find sureties for good behaviour during the rest of his life. The incident here described is mentioned in the *Dictionary of National Biography* entry on Annet, and appears to represent a well-meaning attempt by Goldsmith to find work for a colleague having a hard time. Welsh's account is uncharacteristically lively and is obviously a quotation, but he does not give the source. — T.

[2] Thomas Warton (1728-90), literary historian, was Professor of Poetry at Oxford from 1757 to 1767 and afterwards Poet Laureate. — T.

of young Newbery's schoolfellows at Merchant Taylors' School, who had been a twelvemonth before him at that college, dined with them on the first day. The party, who were all naturally cheerful and well acquainted, were soon at their ease. In the course of the evening, Mr Warton took out of his pocket a linen cap, striped, which terminated in a point, and, pulling off his wig, popped it on his head. The oddity and singularity of his appearance excited a burst of laughter, and a curiosity to know of what this was the symbol, when he informed them that a party of wags had established a club called 'The Jelly Bag Society,' of which this was worn as the token at their meetings, and that it had arisen from the following epigram written by his friend there, Mr Newbery:—

> One day in Chelsea Meadows walking,
> Of poetry and such things talking,
>   Says Ralph — a merry wag —
> 'An epigram, if smart and good
> In all its circumstances should
>   Be like a Jelly Bag!'
>
> 'Your simile, I own, is new,
> But how wilt make it out?' says Hugh.
>   Quoth Ralph: 'I'll tell thee, friend:
> Make it at top both large and fit
> To hold a budget full of wit,
>   And point it at the end!'[1]

"The old gentleman," continues his son, "blushed, and said he did not know how they should have discovered him as the writer, but acknowledged that it was so. Mr Warton observed that the epigram had been ascribed to himself and

---

[1] This first appeared in *The Student*, 1750.— W.

It was also in the *Collection of Pretty Poems for Children Three Foot High*, by Thomas Tagg, Esq., 1756.— T.

others of the club, and that any of them would have been proud to own such a production. This was truly *laudari a laudato viro.* [1]

"Where the Oxford Jelly Bag Society met was a secret in the University, and in order that it should remain so, except to the members, it was held at different places. Curiosity, at last, gave rise to a bet, and the person who was to make the discovery, presuming upon Tom Warton's propensity to attend any drollery or public show, hired a man with a drum to go with him up and down the streets, which drew the people around them, and a noise and hubbub of course. Mr Warton could not resist this, and as the drummer went by the Cross Inn, he started up at the window, and was caught in the Jelly Bag cap! Mr Warton was Francis Newbery's tutor while at Oxford University."

In 1764 Newbery, with T. Greenough, of Ludgate Street, apothecary, and T. Fryer, of Bishopsgate, linen-draper, took out a patent for a machine of new construction for "printing, staining and colouring silk stuffs, linens, cottons, leather and paper by means of engraved copper cylinders, on which the colours are laid by smaller cylinders, which are put in motion by other plain cylinders, and the whole work of filling in, cleaning off, and stamping the impressions, performed by the joynt assistance of sundry springs, and the intermediums of coggs and rings." Whether this machine was ever made of practical use or not we do not know; it probably did not become of commercial importance, but the principle of its construction seems in some sort to foreshadow the present methods of colour printing.

The years 1765 and 1766 saw the publication of the famous *Goody Two-Shoes, Giles Gingerbread,* and many other of his celebrated books, which were inscribed by

---

[1] Roughly, "to be praised by the praiseworthy." — T.

their old friend in St Paul's Churchyard to all young gentlemen and ladies who were good or intended to be good.

But the busy hand and active brain were soon to be quieted for ever, and in the zenith of his fame and prosperity he was overtaken by death. His son, Francis, was summoned from Oxford in the latter part of 1767 suddenly to London, in consequence of his father's severe illness. Newbery's old friend, Dr James, had been constantly attending him for some [time], but his constitution, which never was robust, was now too much broken to be restored. He declined gradually and sank under his complaint on December 22 following, at the comparatively early age of 54. It was not until the month of October in this same year that failing health warned him that it was necessary for him to make his testamentary dispositions, in which he made some slight changes by a codicil to his will in November. During his last illness he occupied himself with drawing up lengthy and minute instructions with reference to the future conduct of his business, for the guidance of his stepson, Thomas Carnan, who was still his right-hand man, chiefly in the retail department, and his nephew, Francis, who was more associated with the publishing business.[1] This document is dated Canbury House, Islington, November 14, 1767.

He was buried by his own request in the churchyard at his birthplace in Waltham St Lawrence, and upon his tomb is the following epitaph, which was written by the Rev. C. Hunter, author of the life of Christopher Smart to which reference has been previously made:—

Stay, Passenger, and contemplate
Virtues, which arose on this spot:
Urbanity that adorned society,

---

[1] See previous footnote (page 77, No.1). — T.

Knowledge that instructed it,
Industry, that raised a family to affluence,
Sagacity, that discerned, and
Skill that introduced
The most powerful discovery
In the annals of Medicine,[1]

The humble wisdom that taught,
And still teaches, moral lessons
To the rising generation.

Lament!
That a Breath inspired with such Virtues is sunk in dust.

Rejoice!
That, through Christ, it is immortal!

---

[1] This doubtless refers to Dr James's Fever Powder. — W.

CHAPTER IV

John Newbery's Character—Described by Dr Johnson as Jack Whirler—Some Lessons of his Career.

"FEW MEN," says his son Francis, "have died more generally or more sincerely lamented. All the newspapers of the time spontaneously burst forth in expressions of commendation of his character and of regret at his loss, which was considered as premature, as he was only fifty-four years of age. He was of an active and cheerful disposition, possessing a fund of natural humour and a most benevolent heart, which indeed carried him into excess, for he was so indiscriminate in his charities that he never passed a beggar without bestowing something. In his address he was polite, and in his manners and conversation so agreeable that he seemed to have been born and bred a gentleman. He was scarcely ever seen without a book or pen in his hand, and his mind was ever occupied for some good purpose. With such qualities, he could not fail to be beloved by all who knew him, and he ranked among his friends men of the first literary talents. As, from the multiplicity of his concerns, he was apt to be forgetful of his engagements, the great author, Dr Johnson, who had often ridiculed this propensity, made him the subject of one of his essays in *The Idler* under the humorous character of 'Jack Whirler.' The delineation was, as it may be supposed, rather a caricature than a portrait, but the likeness in some of the features was just and appropriate." The publication was taken in good part by John Newbery, who, however, threatened to return the compliment by depicting the Doctor, with his peculiarities, in a subsequent number.[1]

In case, however, the over-fond partiality of a son should place his character in too rosy a light, or the gentle banter of Dr Johnson be not quite truthful, it may be well to see what testimony others who knew him have borne to his worth. The oft-quoted paragraph from *The Vicar of Wakefield*, which perhaps has helped as much as anything to keep Newbery's name alive and his memory fresh to all generations, must be cited in this connection. The good Dr Primrose, it will be remembered, on his errand of reclaiming a lost child to virtue, found himself at a little alehouse by the roadside, where he fell ill and languished for near three weeks, and on his recovery was unprovided with money to defray the expenses of his entertainment.

"It is possible," says he, "the anxiety from the last circumstance alone might have brought on a relapse had I not been supplied by a traveller who stopped to take a cursory sort of refreshment. This person was no other than the philanthropic bookseller in St Paul's Churchyard, who has written so many little books for children. He called himself their friend, but he was the friend of all mankind. He was no sooner alighted but he was in haste to be gone, for he was ever on business of the utmost importance, and was at the time actually compiling materials for the history of one Mr Thomas Trip. I immediately recollected this good-natured man's red pimpled face, for he had published for me against the Deuterogamists of the age, and from him I borrowed a few pieces to be paid at my return."

---

[1] He never did so, being no doubt too busy. — T.

Of his goodness and generosity there are abundant examples. It was ever a favourite topic with Oliver Goldsmith to tell pleasant stories of Newbery, who, he said, was the patron of more distressed authors than any man of his time; and that Goldsmith had a high opinion of Newbery is made further evident from the following charade which he wrote:

> What we say of a thing which is just come in fashion
>   And that which we do with the dead
> Is the name of the honestest man in creation;
>   What more of a man can be said?

In Hunter's life of Christopher Smart, who was a contemporary of Francis Newbery's at Cambridge[1] and who spent a great part of his vacations at Mr Newbery's house in St Paul's Churchyard, we find the following with reference to Newbery's kindness to the unfortunate poet, of whom we have given some details in a former chapter:

> The author of these pages gives his testimony with peculiar pleasure to the merits of a gentleman whose friendship and civilities he experienced in early life, and whose beneficence indeed, to say nothing of his intellectual powers, suffered no object within the sphere of their exertions to be uncheered by his kindness.

Hunter further refers to him as a "man of genius and a liberal patron of genius in others," and tells us that Smart "must have been much embarrassed in circumstances but for the kind friendship and assistance of Newbery." Newbery was also characterized by Sir John Hawkins, Johnson's early friend and first biographer, as "a man of a projecting head, a good understanding, and great integrity, who by a fortunate connection with Dr James, the physician, and the honest exertions of his own industry, became the founder of

---

[1] Hunter, not Smart, was the contemporary of Francis Newbery. — T.

a family."[1] But it is said that no man's character can be properly gauged by his contemporaries. Every man has some friends, and fortunate indeed is he who can go through the world without making some enemies and finding some detractors. Newbery, like other men, encountered both. But friends and enemies are alike prone to misjudge and to take false views. It is only as time goes on that the mists roll away, and we are able to look back through an atmosphere purified from passion, feeling and prejudice, that a proper estimate can be formed of the character of an individual.

Nearly all later writers who have referred to Newbery have taken their cue from his contemporaries, most of whom have nothing but good to say of him. Prior, in his *Life of Goldsmith*, says he was "known for his probity, good sense, and a benevolent disposition. His ingenuity and amiable qualities rendered him generally respected. Writers of the first character sought his acquaintance, and in his friendship not unfrequently found occasional alleviation of their most pressing wants." Washington Irving, however, in *Oliver Goldsmith: a Biography* [1849], takes a somewhat more independent view. Newbery, he says, "was a worthy, intelligent, kind-hearted man, and a reasonable, though cautious, friend to authors, relieving them with small loans when in pecuniary difficulties, though always taking care to be well repaid by the labour of their pens." Again Irving, referring to Newbery's death, speaks of him as "Goldsmith's old friend, though frugal-handed employer, of picture-book renown. The poet has celebrated him as the friend of all mankind; he certainly lost nothing by his friendship. He coined the brains of authors in the times of their exigency, and made them pay dear for the plank put out to keep them

---

[1] *The Life of Samuel Johnson, Ll.D,* by Sir John Hawkins (1787) was at first successful, but was eclipsed by Boswell. By "a man of a projecting head" Hawkins meant "a man whose head was full of projects." – T.

from drowning. It is not likely his death caused much lamentation among the scribbling tribe: we may express decent respect for the memory of the just, but we shed tears only at the grave of the generous."

Every other record of him that we have been able to find speaks of him in very different terms, and the title of "Honest John Newbery," which has been so often applied to him, seems to have been in every way well merited. He was no doubt a keen man of business, cautious in all his doings, and able to make a good bargain; all of them excellent qualities, and by no means incompatible with a kindly and generous disposition, although it may be true that they are rarely united.

John Newbery's name must be added to the long and distinguished roll of what are called self-made men, in which he is, we think, entitled to occupy no inconsiderable position. He was almost entirely self-educated, and that, too, after his schooldays were over; for the mere rudiments of learning that he acquired at the village school at Waltham St Lawrence, over a hundred and fifty years ago, could not have fitted him to enter upon the situation he did soon after he went to Reading; and he went on through life adding to his stock of knowledge, reading and studying the best books for this purpose.

The story of his life shows, as that of so many others has done, that it is not necessary to be born in any particular station of life in order to secure success, honour, and troops of friends, and it "should stimulate youths to apply themselves diligently to right pursuits, sparing neither labour nor pains nor self-denial in prosecuting them, and to rely on their own efforts in life rather than depend upon the help or patronage of others. . . the duty of helping one's self in the highest sense involves the helping of one's neighbours."[1]

---

[1] Smiles's *Self-Help.* — W.

That he was fortunate in his career there is no doubt. But "fortune favours the brave." If he had not worked hard at his books while at home at Waltham, he would never have qualified himself to succeed to the business of Carnan, and thus to lay the foundation of his success. Good fortune is of comparatively little use without hard work, and John Newbery never spared himself. He is another example of what untiring energy, indomitable perseverance, and enthusiastic love of work can do. He sought the right groove for his talents with unremitting zeal, and when he had found it he applied himself vigorously to work in it.

CHAPTER V

Newbery's Will—Dissensions between the Newberys and Carnan, and
Rupture of Business Relations—The Successors in the Business—Abraham
Badcock—John Harris—T. Carnan and the Almanacs.

THE provisions of John Newbery's will were unfortunately
somewhat complicated, and things soon began to work
inharmoniously among his successors after his death.

To his son Francis he left the medicines and the medicine
business for his sole profit; and directed that he, with [John
Newbery's] stepson, Thomas Carnan, and his nephew,
Francis Newbery, should carry on the general [bookselling,
publishing &c.] business for their joint interest and benefit,
securing proper provision for his widow and his
stepdaughter, Mrs Smart, wife of the poet. Young Francis, the
son, was, we should imagine, from many of the records he
has left behind him, a person of no small importance in his
own estimation, and somewhat pompous and dictatorial in
manner. These characteristics, added to the fact that he was
entirely without business training and experience, led to a
very uncomfortable condition of things. Immediately on John
Newbery's death (in 1767) Francis, the nephew, opened a
shop and began to publish books at 20 Ludgate Street, while
F. Newbery the son and T. Carnan continued at 65 St Paul's
Churchyard. The following imprint of an edition of a *New*

The premises at the corner of St Paul's
Churchyard occupied by Francis Newbery
the nephew and his successors

No. 45 St Paul's Churchyard: the
new building to which Francis the
son moved the medicine business
in 1779

History of England, published in 1772, shows that there was no concealment of the far from cordial feelings that animated the rival firms:—

> London, printed for T. Carnan and F. Newbery, Junior, at No. 65, in St Paul's Church Yard (but not for F.Newbery, at the corner of Ludgate Street, who has no share in the late Mr John Newbery's Books for Children).

On the back of the title, facing a dedication to "To the Young Gentlemen and Ladies of Great Britain and Ireland," is the following notice:—

> The Public are desired to observe that F.Newbery, at the Corner of St Paul's Church Yard and Ludgate Street, has not the least Concern in any of the late Mr John Newbery's Entertaining Books for Children; and to prevent having paltry Compilations obtruded on them, instead of Mr John Newbery's useful Publications, they are desired to be particularly careful to apply for them to T. Carnan and F. Newbery, jun. (Successors to the late Mr John Newbery) at No. 65, near the Bar in St Paul's Church Yard.

But Carnan and Newbery were not themselves on good terms; the former thought he was hardly treated by the elder Newbery's will, and that he ought to have had a larger share in the business which he had so greatly helped to make, and he, too, began trading on his own account.

No. 20 Ludgate Street is the site of the establishment at the corner of St Paul's Churchyard now [1885] occupied by the successors of the Newberys.[1] Here were four houses, according to the deeds "bounded on the north by the mansion-house of the prebendary and penitentiary and a house named the 'Curlews' which were next the palace

---

[1] Properly speaking, the successors of Francis Newbery the nephew and his widow Elizabeth. — T.

garden of the Bishop of London." The whole place was (I quote the deeds again) "burned down and consumed in the dreadful fire which happened in London in the month of September, Anno Domini 1666." The houses, which then belonged to the prebend of St Pancras, were rebuilt after the fire, and remained until they were pulled down and again rebuilt in 1885. Francis, the nephew, continued to publish books here until he died in January 1780. The *Gentleman's Magazine* bore his imprint from the year 1767.[1] His widow, Elizabeth Newbery, carried on the business there after his death. After some years she retired therefrom, drawing out of it, until her death in 1821 at the age of 75, a yearly allowance of £500, and John Harris, who had long managed the business for her, succeeded to it.[2]

John Harris was formerly an apprentice to Evans the bookseller, with whom Goldsmith had an affray in 1773 in respect of a libel in the *London Packet,* of which Evans was the publisher. Harris witnessed the affair, of which the following account is given in the *London Chronicle*, March 27-30, 1773:— "Dr Goldsmith, supposing himself ill-treated by a letter in the *London Packet,* went to the person's shop who published the paper, and struck him on the back with his cane. A scuffle ensued, in which the publisher made

---

[1] In the account books of Benjamin Collins, Salisbury, I find the following entry in the book kept by him entitled "an account of copies, their cost and value": "The *Gentleman's Magazine,* 8vo, one twelfth share, bought of Messrs D. Henry and R. Cave, January 1, 1755, for £333. 6s. 8d."; and a subsequent entry in red ink, "sold to F. Newbery." — W.

(The *Gentleman's Magazine,* founded by Edward Cave in 1731, ran until 1914. Dr Johnson was at one time a regular contributor. — T.)

[2] For some time before Harris, Mr Abraham Badcock, who died April 18, 1797, appears to have managed the business for Mrs Newbery. His judgment of books was said to have been good, and he possessed literary talents. A few of the best designed books for children were written by him at moments of leisure. — W.

uncommon use of his nails, and was at length knocked down; he then arose, seized a stool and attacked his antagonist, till, some people coming in, they were parted. Thus ended the contest between the son of literature and the publisher, the latter of whom bears a black eye and the author a scratched face."

Carnan and Newbery [the son] continued to issue books with their joint imprint until about the year 1782, and Carnan's name appears alone in the London directories as at 65 St Paul's Churchyard down to 1788.

"The reputation of Thomas Carnan is associated with more durable records than the obituary of the *Gentleman's Magazine*" [writes Charles Knight in *Shadows of the old Booksellers*, London, 1865, pp. 244-246.] "He lives in the eloquence of Erskine.[1]

"John Newbery died in 1767, and soon after Carnan entered upon the business in St Paul's Churchyard, he became possessed with a very sensible notion that the Stationers' Company had no legal title to their monopoly of almanacs. He began, therefore, to publish almanacs of his own.[2] The company, after having anathematized him as the base publisher of 'counterfeit almanacs,' sent him to prison on a summary process as regularly as he issued his annual commodities. A friend of his family told me, some forty years ago, that this incorrigible old bookseller always at this season kept a clean shirt in his pocket, that he might make a decent appearance before the magistrate and the keeper of Newgate. But Carnan persevered till the judges of the Court of

---

[1] Thomas Erskine (1750-1823), famous advocate and later Lord Chancellor. He was under 30 and at the beginning of his career when he appeared for Carnan at the bar of the House of Commons in the case referred to here. — T.

[2] The Stationers' Company, which received a royal charter in 1557, was an association of printers which controlled the trade for many years. By the eighteenth century, its power was waning. — T.

Common Pleas decided against the validity of the patent, and an injunction which had been obtained in the Exchequer was immediately dissolved. The Stationers' Company then induced Lord North to bring a Bill into Parliament to revest in them the monopoly that had been declared illegal. In 1779 Erskine, in a speech which remains as one of the great triumphs of his oratory, procured the rejection of this Bill by a large majority.

"Carnan, who had become the proprietor of *The Traveller,* published by John Newbery, opposed the republication of Goldsmith's poems in the booksellers' edition of 1779. He was at issue with the leaders of the trade. 'It is much to be regretted,' says Mr Cunningham in his preface to Johnson's *Lives of the Poets* [1854], 'that the petty interest of a bookseller named Carnan should have excluded Goldsmith from the number of his *Lives.'* There was evidently something more than 'petty interest' which set Carnan in opposition to the great body of his fellows. The great question was in hot dispute in 1777. The Stationers had the ear of the Prime Minister; but Carnan was in confidential intercourse with Erskine."

Francis Newbery, the son, relinquished the book publishing and confined himself to the medicine business alone soon after he went to his new house at the north-east end of St Paul's in 1779, and by some means or other, either by transfer or purchase, or revival of lapsed books, all the old publications of Newbery subsequently passed into the hands of Elizabeth (his cousin's widow) and to Harris and his successors.[1]

---

[1]This is questionable. Elizabeth Newbery does not appear to have published any John Newbery title. — T.

CHAPTER VI

Books for Children in the Reign of Queen Anne—Chapbooks and Chapmen—John Newbery's Books—Their Style and Authorship—Leigh Hunt—Southey—Scarcity of Juvenile Books for the Period—Newbery's Ingenious Methods of Advertising—Piracies of his Books.

THE LITERATURE provided for children before John Newbery began to make it his business to cater specially for them was of the very scantiest character. Mr John Ashton, in his interesting book, *Social Life in the Reign of Queen Anne*, however, tells us that even in the early days of the last [eighteenth] century the little folk had their special literature. "For," he says, "there was compiled and printed 'a play-book for children, to allure them to read as soon as they can speak plain; composed of small pages so as not to tire children; printed with a fair and pleasing letter, the matter and method plainer and easier than any yet extant.' The price of this was fourpence, and it must have been a favourite, for it is advertised as being in its second edition in 1703. Certainly the little ones then lacked many advantages in this way that ours now possess; but, on the other hand, so much was not required of them. There was no dreaded 'examination' to prepare for — no doing lessons all day long and then working hard at night to get ready for the next day's toil. They were not taught half a dozen languages, and all the ologies, while still in the nursery; but, were the suggestions and advice given to 'the Mother' in Steele's 'Lady's Library' thoroughly carried out, they would grow up good men and women. The boys, however, had strong meat provided for them in such tales as 'Jack and the Giants' &c. Steele, in the *Tatler,* No. 95, says, speaking of a little boy of eight years old, 'I perceived him a very great historian in *Aesop's Fables,* but he frankly declared to me his mind, "that he did not delight in that learning, because he did not believe they were true," for which reason I found he had very much turned his studies for about a twelvemonth past into the *Lives and Adventures of Don Bellianis of Greece, Guy of Warwick, The Seven Champions,* and other historians of that age. . . He would tell you the mismanagements of John Hickathrift, find fault with the passionate temper in *Bevis of Southampton,* and loved Saint George for being the champion of England. . . I was extolling his accomplishments when her mother told me that the little girl who led me in this morning was in her way a better scholar than he. "Betty," says she, "deals chiefly in Fairies and Sprights, and sometimes in a winter night will terrify the maids with her accounts until they are afraid to go up to bed." '

"In all probability the child learned his letters in the first instance from a horn book such as were then commonly used and sold — as the following excerpt from an advertisement shows: 'Joseph Hazard, at the Bible, in Stationer's Court, near Ludgate, sells. . . Spelling books, Primers, Horn-books, &c.' Horn books are now very scarce indeed, and the man lucky enough to possess a genuine one must feel proud of his rarity. It consisted of a small sheet of paper, generally about 4in. by 3in. or so — sometimes smaller — on which was printed the alphabet, both in capitals and small text, the vowels, and a few simple combinations, such as ab, eb, ob, ab — ba, be, bi, bo, bu, &c., and the Lord's Prayer. This was laid on a flat piece of board with a roughly shaped handle, and covered with a thin plate of horn, fastened to the board by copper tacks driven through an edging of thin copper. It therefore would stand a vast amount of rough usage before it would be destroyed — a fact of great importance in elementary education."[1]

Newbery was the first publisher who introduced the regular system of a Juvenile Library, and gave children books in a more permanent form than the popular chapbooks of the period. Before the beginning of the present [nineteenth] century, the whole of the country was systematically travelled by a class of hawkers who, besides carrying small articles for domestic and personal use and adornment, traded in ballads, almanacs, and similar literary wares. These wandering tradesmen were called chapmen, and the little books they carried are known as chapbooks. These were, it will readily be supposed, rude in execution and crude in their literary style, but they occupy a distinct place in the history of the literature of the people. Mr John Ashton, in his *Chapbooks of the Eighteenth Century,* gives an excellent insight into the character of this class of literature, which, with the exception of certain dreary religious books, furnished the staple literary food of the young people of the eighteenth century.

The books issued by Newbery were more durable than these chapbooks, which were simply folded and not stitched, for they were "strongly bound and gilt," and they were, although in many respects far behind the books of today both in mechanical execution and literary quality, of a character in every way more suited to the youthful mind than the coarser productions in chapbook form, or than the religious works to which we have referred. Among these latter are to be found such specimens as *War with the Devil,*

---

[1] The Royal Battledores and other battledores which Collins and Newbery printed and published, and of which they sold enormous numbers, were modifications of the horn book. They were printed on cardboard and folded into three. — W.

or the Young Man's Conflict with the Powers of Darkness (Belfast, 1700), in which, after ninety pages of argument between Youth, Conscience, Truth and the Devil, the young man is converted and the Devil conquered. Then follows an equally dreary *Dialogue between an Old Apostate and a Young Professor,* the Apostate being, of course, a Roman Catholic, who had joined that communion in James II's time. The language is of the plainest, and it is hard to say whether the apostate or the Professor is the more objectionable. Then we have Burton's *Youth's Divine Pastime,* in which forty scripture histories are versified and illustrated with cuts. Many of them are on subjects which we do not usually teach our children and which we have banished from the prayer-book lessons in public reading. It was a more plain-spoken age, and Burton sets forth the facts of the stories in a most unvarnished manner. It was from these, and such as these, that John Newbery arose to deliver the children of his day, and in reading the titles of some of his earlier books it is at once seen that a new note has been struck, and a new field opened for culture and development.

"There is nothing more remarkable in Mr Newbery's little books than the originality of their style. There have been attempts to approach its simplicity — its homeliness. Great authors have tried their hands at imitating its clever adaptation to the childish intellect, but they have failed. Never was failure more complete than that of Sir Walter Scott [in *The Tales of a Grandfather.*] He could not sustain the difficult task of writing in the way of his prototypes, Mr Newbery and Mr Griffith Jones. They could carry the union of puerility and instruction through these volumes. . . The child's play was work too hard for him."[1]

The didactic and tiresome style of the writers of the "age

---

[1] *Shadows of the Old Booksellers,* by Charles Knight, London, 1865, pp. 240-41. — W.

of prose and reason" is naturally reflected in many of Newbery's little books, and some of them contain coarsenesses of expression which would be very shocking to the parents and guardians of the present day, but they were all written with a good intent, and though they seldom appeared with an author's name there is little doubt that many of the clever and distinguished men whom Newbery had drawn around him had a hand in their compilation.

Many are said to have been written by Newbery himself, and there is every reason to believe that the same hand which drew up the ingenious advertisements and quaint title-pages of some of them is responsible for the contents of the little books. Many were originated though not written by Benjamin Collins, the Salisbury printer.

Mr Forster in his life of Goldsmith says: "I believe that to Newbery himself the great merit is due of having first sought to reform in some material point the moral of these books. He did not thrust all naughty boys into the jaws of the dragon, nor elevate all good boys to ride in King Peppin's coach. Goldsmith. . . said, more than once, that he had a hankering to write for children; and if he had realized his intention of composing the fables in which little fishes and other creatures should talk, our children's libraries would have had one rich possession the more."

I am strongly inclined to believe that Goldsmith really did gratify this hankering, and had much more to do with Newbery's books for children than has been credited to him. In the preface to the facsimile reprint of *Goody Two-Shoes* [Griffith & Farran, 1881] I have discussed fully the reasons why I attribute that book to him.[1]

Washington Irving, in his life of Goldsmith (p.101), says,

---

[1] Mr J.M.W. Gibbs, in his new edition of Goldsmith [1884] attributes the preface only to him, and is disposed to believe that the book is by another hand, probably that of Newbery himself. — W.

It is suggested, and with great probability, that he wrote for Mr Newbery the famous nursery story of *Goody Two-Shoes,* which appeared in 1765, at a moment when Goldsmith was scribbling for Newbery, and much pressed for funds. Several quaint little titles introduced in his Essays show that he had a turn for this species of mock history; and the advertisement and title page bear the stamp of his sly and playful humour. . .

Of these [books with the Newbery imprint] many writers have spoken in loving recollection. . . Leigh Hunt, in his book *The Town* [1848] says:— "But the most illustrious of all booksellers in our boyish days, not for his great names, not for his dinners, not for his riches that we know of, not for any other full-grown celebrity, but for certain little penny books, radiant with gold and rich with bad pictures, was Mr Newbery, the famous children's bookseller, 'at the corner of St Paul's Churchyard,' next Ludgate Street. The house is still occupied by a successor, and children may have books there as formerly, but not the same.

"The gilding, we confess, we regret: gold, somehow, never looked so well as in adorning literature. The pictures also — may we own that we preferred the uncouth coats, the staring blotted eyes, and round pieces of rope for hats, of our very badly drawn contemporaries, to all the proprieties of modern embellishment?"[1]

Mr Samuel Phillips, in his *Essay on Robert Southey,*[2] tells us that "as soon as the child (Southey) could read, his aunt's friends furnished him with literature. The son of Newbery of

---

[1] There was no Mr Newbery at the corner of St Paul's Churchyard in Hunt's childhood. Assuming that he remembered the address correctly, the establishment he patronized would have been that of Elizabeth Newbery, widow of Francis the nephew. Hunt was born in 1784; Francis died in 1780. The successor he referred to would have (in 1848) have been the firm of Grant & Griffith, afterwards Griffith & Farran (see page 157.) — T.

[2] *Essays from 'The Times,'* Vol. 1 (London, revised edn, 1871.) — T.

St Paul's Churchyard, and the well-known publisher of *Goody Two-Shoes, Giles Gingerbread,* and 'other such delectable histories in sixpenny books for children, splendidly bound in the flowered and gilt Dutch paper of former days, sent the child twenty such volumes, and laid the foundation of a love of books which grew with the child's growth and did not cease in age, even when the vacant mind and eye could only gaze in piteous though blissful imbecility upon the things they loved."

Malcolm in his *Londinium Redivivum*[1] says:— "Newbery for many years issued shoals of little useful publications for children; a library which I well remembered possessing when nearly 4,000 miles from England; and I date my first partiality for literature to have arisen from the *splendid bindings and beautiful wood engravings* of Newbery."

Many of these famous little books have doubtless absolutely disappeared. Books for children, above all other, are short-lived and vanish more successfully than any other kind of literature. When they have served their turn and little hands have thumbed and worn them well nigh to pieces, few people think of saving the tattered scraps. Some, however, have fortunately been preserved, but as that genial and kindly book lover, the Rev. Richard Hooper, says:— "Books from 1730 to 1750 are more uncommon than at almost any other period. Both our great university libraries are very deficient in that period, and it was only lately that the British Museum has supplied the deficiency." It is far easier to find seventeenth century books than those of that period of the eighteenth century; a very considerable number will be found catalogued of which we have not been able to find more than the titles in advertisements and lists, and many may have escaped notice altogether owing to the imperfect

---

[1] James Peller Malcolm, *Londinium Redivivum: an antient history and modern description of London,* 4 vols, London 1802-7. — T.

files of newspapers in the British Museum and other public libraries.

A writer in *The World,* No. 115, March 13, 1755, in a somewhat satirical paper on the tricks of advertising of his day, more especially in connection with the "gentlemen of the faculty" or "practitioners in physic," jocularly proposes to dispose of the volumes of *The World* at 3s. per volume, declaring that "to relieve the unhappy is the full end of this publication," and continues:—

I had written thus far when I received a visit from a friend, who, upon my acquainting him with the public-spirited scheme which I have here laid before my readers, shook his head and told me that an author of his acquaintance had greatly outdone me in generosity, of which he could convince me in an hour's time. He then left me abruptly, without so much as waiting for an answer, and in less than the time promised sent me the following advertisement cut out of a newspaper:— 'This day was published *Nurse Truelove's New Year's Gift, or the book of books for children,* adorned with cuts, and designed as a present for every little boy who would become a great man and ride upon a fine horse, and to every little girl who would become a great woman and ride in a lord-mayor's gilt coach. Printed for the author, who has ordered these books to be given gratis to all little boys and girls, at the Bible and Sun in St Paul's Churchyard, they paying for the binding, which is only twopence each book.'

I confess very freely that the generosity of this advertisement put me a little out of countenance; but as I pique myself upon nothing so much as my benevolence to mankind, I soon came to a resolution not to be outdone by this public-spirited gentleman; and I hereby give notice that the above-mentioned three volumes of *The World,* together with a very elaborate index to each (all of which were, I confess, intended to be sold), will now be given gratis at every bookseller's shop in town, to all sorts of persons, *they only paying* NINE SHILLINGS *for the binding.*

Newbery was probably one of the most ingenious advertisers of his day, and his ingenuity was in most cases rewarded with success. He was almost as great in the art of puffing his wares as the immortal Puff himself,[1] and he employed the puff of every kind: "the puff direct, the puff preliminary, the puff collateral, the puff collusive, and the puff oblique, or puff by implication" were all used in their turn, and no little skill was displayed in their concoction. We have before us a circular addressed "To the Minister, Churchwardens, and Overseers of the Poor of the Parish of ——," dated from "the Bible and Sun in St Paul's Churchyard, opposite the north door of the church," June 7, 1751, advising them, with a view to keeping down the rates by preventing sickness among the poor, to use Dr James's fever powders, and quoting a reduced price for those who buy them for such a charitable purpose.

Newbery had well learned the lesson of the following lines:

> New books we know require a puff,
> A title to entrap the eyes
> And catch the reader by surprise,

and it may be interesting to give some specimens of how he applied his knowledge. The following are some of his methods of announcing his little books and keeping them before the world:—

Penny Morning Post, June 18, 1744

According to Act of Parliament (neatly bound and gilt), a *Little Pretty Pocket Book,* intended for the instruction and amusement of little Master Tommy and pretty Miss Polly; with an agreeable letter to each from *Jack the Giant Killer;* as also a *Ball and Pincushion,* the use of which will infallibly make Tommy a good boy and Polly a good girl. To the whole is prefixed a letter on education, humbly

---

[1] The 'practitioner in panegyric' in Sheridan's play *The Critic* (1779).— T.

addressed to all parents, guardians, governesses &c., wherein rules are laid down for making their children *strong, healthy, virtuous, wise, and happy.*

> Children, like tender Oziers, take the bow,
> And as they first are fashioned, always grow. — DRYDEN.

> Just as the twig is bent the tree's inclined;
> 'Tis education forms the vulgar mind. — POPE.

Printed for J. Newbery at the Bible and Crown, near Devereux Court, without Temple Bar. Price of the Book, 6d; with a Ball and Pincushion, 8d.

Mar. 1, 1751

To all little good boys and girls.

My dear Friends,—You are desired not to be uneasy that the publication of your *Lilliputian Magazine* is deferred till Saturday. The whole is printed, and all the servants of the Society are employed in making them up for you, but as the number is so large, 'twill be impossible to get them perfected before that time.—

I am, my dear Friends, yours affectionately,

R. Goodwill, Secretary.

From my Office at the Bible and Sun
in St Paul's Churchyard,
Feb. 28, 1751.

March 17, 1759

To the Parents, Guardians, and Governesses of Great Britain and Ireland.

At a time when all complain of the depravity of human nature, and the corrupt principles of mankind, any design that is calculated to remove the evils, and enforce a contrary contract, will undoubtedly deserve the attention and encouragement of the publick.

It has been said, and said wisely, that the only way to remedy these evils is to begin with the rising generation, and to take the mind in its infant state, when it is uncorrupted and susceptible of any impression; to represent their duties and future interest in a manner that shall seem rather intended to amuse than instruct, to excite their attention with images and pictures that are familiar and pleasing; to warm their affections with such subjects as are capable of giving them delight, and of impressing on their tender minds proper sentiments of religion, justice, honour, and virtue.

> When infant reason grows apace, it calls
> For the kind hand of an assiduous care;
> Delightful task! To rear the tender thought,
> To teach the young idea how to shoot,
> To pour the fresh instruction o'er the mind,
> To breather th'inspiring spirit, to implant
> The generous purpose in the glowing breast.
>   —THOMSON.

How far Mr *Newbery's* little books may tend to forward this good work may be, in some measure, seen by what are already published, and, it is presumed, will more evidently appear by others which are now in the press.

The books published for the instruction and amusement of children are as follow, which are all adorned with cuts and bound and gilt.

These books are sold by J. Newbery, at the Bible and Sun, in St Paul's Church-yard, opposite the north door of the church, where great allowances are made to those who buy quantities to sell again.

In the *London Chronicle* for December 19–January 1, 1765, the following advertisement appeared:—

The Philosophers, Politicians, Necromancers, and the learned in every faculty are desired to observe that on the 1st of January, being New Year's day (oh, that we may all lead new lives!) Mr Newbery intends to publish the following important volumes, bound and gilt, and hereby invites all his little friends who are good to call for them at the Bible and Sun in St Paul's Church-yard, but those who are naughty to have none.

Another means which Newbery employed to make his books and other wares known was by bringing in allusions to them in the text of the stories. Everyone who has read *Goody Two-Shoes* will recall the incident of little Margery's father's death; he was "seized with a violent fever in a place where Dr James's Fever Powder was not to be had, and where he died miserably." In the same book we find, "She then sung the 'Cuz's Chorus' (which may be found in the *Little Pretty Plaything*, published by Mr Newbery)." Again, "We have already informed the reader the school where she taught was that which was before kept by Mrs Williams, whose character you may find in my *New Year's Gift*." And at the end of the same book we find, "The books usually read by the scholars of Mrs Two Shoes are these, and are sold at Mr Newbery's, at the Bible and Sun in St Paul's Church-yard."

In another little book, *Fables in Verse*, the following occurs: "Woglog at Bath. Lady:— 'Well, Mr Woglog, where have you been?' 'At church, Madam; and pray, my lady, where have *you* been?' 'Drinking the waters,' said she. 'But not for health?' 'No, truly; I only drink them for wantonness.' 'Well, Madam, and have they cured you of that complaint?' says Mr Woglog. The lady blushed and took a turn on the Grand Parade, while Woglog stept into Mr Leake's to read one of Mr Newbery's little books."

In the *Blossoms of Morality*, the chapter entitled "The Book of Nature" opens thus:— "My dear Papa," said young Theophilus to his father, "I cannot help pitying those poor little boys whose parents are not in a condition to purchase them such a nice gilded library as that with which you have supplied me from my good friends at the corner of St Paul's Churchyard. Surely such unhappy boys must be very ignorant all their lives, for what can they learn without books?"

The father, while agreeing, points out that there is room for infinite study in the "Book of Nature."[1]

From *The Twelfth Day Gift* (1767), we cull the following examples of the puff direct:— Page 5 — "Pulling Mr Newbery's *New Year's Gift* out of his pocket, he read." Page 24 — "Read the following character from the *Lilliputian Magazine.*" Page 41 — "Turned to the poems published by Mr Newbery for children of six feet high." Page 88 — "Pulled one of Mr Newbery's books out of his pocket." Page 94 refers to *The Newtonian Philosophy, &c.,* by J. Newbery. Page 127 — "Taking Mr Newbery's *Valentine's Gift* out of her pocket."

These little books were many of them published by the King's authority, which was the manner in which copyright was secured at that period, as witness the following announcement from the *Mercurius Latinus,* Augusti 9, 1746:—

GEORGE the Second, by the Grace of God, King of Great Britain, &c., to all whom these presents shall concern, Greeting. Whereas our trusty and well-beloved *John Newbery of London,* Bookseller, hath, with great expence and much labour, compiled a work intitled *The Circle of the Sciences; or, The Compendious Library,* digested in a method entirely new, whereby each branch of *Polite Literature* is rendered extremely easy and instructive. We, being willing to encourage all works of public benefit, are graciously pleased to grant him our royal privilege and licence for the sole printing, publishing, and vending the same.

> *Given at St James', the 8th of December 1744,*
> *by His Majesty's Command,*
> *Holles Newcastle.*

---

[1] *Blossoms of Morality* was not in fact a John Newbery title — it was published in 1789 by Elizabeth Newbery, widow of Francis the nephew — and the priggishness of the extract quoted is characteristic of a growing trend in the latter years of the century. — T.

But owing to the laxness of the copyright laws at that period, or possibly to the fact that Newbery did not renew his licences when they expired, many of the books were pirated by printers in York, Newcastle, Dublin, and other provincial towns, and often in terribly mutilated and travestied forms. Although the foundation of the present system of copyright was made in April 1710, it was not until 1769 that the construction of the Act of Queen Anne by the House of Lords in a celebrated case practically laid down the law.

A notable instance of these piracies is that of *The Idler,* respecting which the following extract from Boswell's *Johnson* is interesting:—

This paper (*The Idler*) was in such high estimation before it was collected into volumes that it was seized on with avidity by various publishers of newspapers and magazines, to enrich their publications. Johnson, to put a stop to this unfair proceeding, wrote for the *Universal Chronicle* the following advertisement, in which there is, perhaps, more pomp of words than the occasion demanded:—

"London, Jan. 5, 1759. — Advertisement. — The proprietors of the paper entitled *The Idler,* having found that those essays are inserted in the newspapers and magazines with so little regard to justice or decency that the *Universal Chronicle,* in which they first appear, is not always mentioned, think it necessary to declare to the publishers of those collections that however patiently they have hitherto endured these injuries, made yet more injurious by contempt, they have now determined to endure them no longer. They have already seen essays for which a very large price is paid transferred with the most shameless rapacity into the weekly or monthly compilations, and their right, at least for the present, alienated from them before they could themselves be said to enjoy it. But they would not willingly be thought to want tenderness, even for men by whom no tenderness hath been shewn. The past is without remedy, and shall be without resentment. But those who have been thus busy with their sickles in the fields of their neighbours are henceforth to take notice that the time of impunity is at an end. Whoever shall, without our leave, lay the hand of rapine upon our papers is to expect that we shall vindicate our due by the means which justice prescribes and which are warranted by the immemorial prescriptions of honourable trade. We shall lay hold, in our turn, on their copies, degrade them from the pomp of wide margin and diffuse typography, contract them into a narrow space, and sell them at an humble price; yet not with a view of growing rich with confiscations, for we think not much better of money got by punishment than by crimes. We shall, therefore, when our losses are repaid give what profit shall remain to the Magdalens; for we know not who can be more properly taxed for the support of penitent prostitutes than prostitutes in whom there yet appears neither penitence nor shame."[1]

This tirade of Johnson's shows that the condition of things existing in England at the time he wrote was somewhat akin to that which in the present year of grace 1885 obtains between some of the publishers of England and the United States. His threatened reprisals might almost be taken as a description of what, we regret to say, we have seen some publishers doing, both in this country and on the other side of the Atlantic. May the time soon come when an international copyright law will render such doings impossible.[2]

---

[1] Boswell's *Johnson*, Everyman edition, vol. i. p. 212. — T.

[2] The time did come, though inevitably breaches occur. In 1886, several leading European powers agreed on an international copyright convention (the 'Berne Convention') which was ratified by the UK in November 1887. The USA and countries in Central America set up conventions, principally the Buenos Aires Convention of 1910, based on their own hemisphere. To bridge the gap, the Universal Copyright Convention was formulated in Geneva in 1952. This introduced the copyright line with the symbol © for international protection. — T.

More light is let in upon the way in which literary preserves were poached upon in the last century by the following extract from the preface which Oliver Goldsmith prefixed to his collected Essays:—

> But though they (the essays) have passed pretty silently into the world, I can by no means complain of their circulation. The magazines and papers of the day have indeed been liberal enough in this respect. Most of these essays have been regularly represented twice or thrice a year, and conveyed to the public through the kennel of some engaging compilation. If there be a pride in multiplied editions, I have seen some of my labours sixteen times reprinted, and claimed by different parents as their own. I have seen them flourished at the beginning with praise, and signed at the end with the names of Philautos, Philalethes, Philalutheros, Philanthropos. These gentlemen have kindly stood sponsors to my production, and to flatter me more, have always taken my errors on themselves.
>
> It is time, however, at last to vindicate my claims; and as these entertainers of the public, as they call themselves, have partly lived upon me for some years, let me now try if I cannot live a little upon myself. I would desire, in this case, to imitate that fat man whom I have somewhere heard of in a shipwreck, who when the sailors, pressed by famine, were taking slices from his posteriors to satisfy their hunger, insisted with great justice on having the first cut for himself.

Newbery also felt the effect of these piracies in other cases, for in *Lloyd's Evening Post,* October 2, 1765, the following advertisement appears:—

> As several persons in the printing and bookselling business have, without the least regard to property, honour, or conscience, pirated this Dictionary, and others of Mr Newbery's little books, he hopes all parents and guardians, as well as the young gentlemen and ladies, for whose emolument they were written, will do him the favour and the justice to ask for his books, and observe that his name is prefixed to those they buy, that he, who has entered so

heartily into their service, and been ever studious of their improvement, may, at least, reap some of the fruits of his labour.

If Thomas Green, M.A., should exist in any region below the moon, and Thomas Green, M.A., be really the compiler of the Spelling Dictionary just published, it is a piece of work that Thomas Green, M.A., ought to be ashamed of, as the business was already done to his hands.

The Bookseller, too, if he had not been a booby, or worse, would never have employed Thomas Green, M.A., to write a book which had been written and printed so many years before; and especially while the tenth edition of it was selling before his face with such rapidity.

N.B. — At the Bible and Sun above mentioned may be had all Mr Newbery's little books, new editions of which are now published.

Here is another of Newbery's protests against the piratical practices of his day:—

As some of the people concerned with the 'Ladies' New and Polite Pocket Memorandum Book' had not time to purloin the account of the Duke of Bridgewater's aqueduct from this pocket-book to enrich their own, they have ungenerously thrust it (without any acknowledgment) into a bungled-up magazine; for which the public will undoubtedly despise both them and their performance.

Although Newbery's fame as a publisher is founded mainly on the books for children that he produced, and his connection with Goldsmith, he left no field of literature untried in his publishing ventures. A glance at the catalogue of books he published will show that Theology, Fiction, Prose and Poetry, Scientific and Educational works, Music, and indeed every department of literature is represented, and although the Kindergarten was not then dreamed of, he provided what would now be known in the public elementary schools as a varied occupation for infants in the shape of

A sett of fifty-six squares, with cuts and Directions for playing with them, newly invented for the use of Children.

By which alone, or with very little assistance, they may learn to Spell, Read, Write, make Figures, and cast up any common sum in Arithmetick, before they are old enough to be sent to school, and that by way of Amusement and Diversion. The whole so contrived as to yield as much entertainment as any of their Play Games usually do. By which means a great deal of Time, commonly idled away by Children, will be profitably as well as pleasantly employed.

Upon the plan of the learned Mr Locke, who in his excellent Treatise of Education hath the following words on this method of teaching Children:— "Thus children may be cozen'd into a knowledge of the Letters, be taught to Read, without perceiving it to be anything but a Sport, and play themselves into that which others are whipped for."

To which is added a Collection of Moral and Prudential Maxims intended to instil into their young minds the Principles of Virtue and the knowledge of Mankind.

In the getting-up of these books he seemed to have spared no pains, and to have done his best with the materials of the day. Paper, printing, and binding alike were of the first quality procurable, and some of the little sixpenny volumes are better printed than many of the much more pretentious books of modern times.

The "flowery and gilt" binding of John Newbery's little books, of which he made such a feature in his announcements — and which added so largely to the attractiveness of his publications — is completely a thing of the past, and is as extinct as the Dodo. It was extensively imitated by T. Saint of Newcastle, Marshall, and others, and for a long time was exceedingly popular. An attempt to discover the whereabouts of its manufacture on the Continent (it was called a Dutch paper, but it was made both in Holland and Germany) some few years ago elicited the fact that the demand had long since ceased and the stamps and presses used in its manufacture had been destroyed.

Many novelties and improvements in the get-up of the books in other ways were introduced or adopted by the

Newberys — one of these was the binding "in the vellum manner." The books were half bound, with an open back in green vellum and green paper, and on the inside of the cover was pasted this notice:—

> The Purchasers of Books bound in the Vellum manner are desired to observe that they are sewed much better than the books which are bound in Leather; open easier at the Back, and are not so liable to warp in being read. If by any Accident the Covers should be stained or rubbed they may be new covered for a Penny, an advantage that cannot be remedied in Leather; so that this method of Binding is not only cheaper, but it is presumed will be found more useful.
>
> The only Motive for trying this Experiment was to adopt a Substitute for Leather, which was greatly enhanced in its price, either by an increased Consumption, or of Monopoly; how far that purpose will be answered must be submitted to the Determination of the Reader.

Many of the volumes were so bound, but the plan did not take permanent hold, for it was not long before it was superseded by the more modern cloth binding.

MR & MRS FOLIO AT OXFORD

George Colman the Elder

Riddle-me-ree

from

FOOD *for the* MIND; *or,*
a New RIDDLE-BOOK

FOUR wings I have,
   Which swiftly mount on high
On sturdy pinions,
Yet I never fly;
And tho' my body often moves around,
Upon the self-same spot
I'm always found;
And, like a nurse who chews the infants
   meat,
I chew for man before that he can eat.

Mr & Mrs Folio at Oxford

[This was No. 3 of *Terrae-Filius*, a series of papers published by
Colman during an Encaenia (commemoration of founders and
benefactors) at Oxford which marked the end of the Seven Years'
War in 1763.

Colman (1732-94) is known as the Elder to distinguish him from
his son, George Colman the Younger (1762-1836); both were
dramatists of some note in their day. It is not in doubt that Mr and
Mrs Folio and their son Bonus were the Newberys and their son
Francis, though Colman gave them the skimpy disguise of a fictional
name and caused Mr Folio to refer to Newbery in the third person.
A letter to Colman from David Garrick, dated from Chatsworth a
few days after publication of this number of *Terrae-Filius*, says that
Newbery "deserved correction" but adds that "I am so delicate
about women that I could wish that *she* had been exempted from
the lash."

Colman had aristocratic connections and was the nephew (some
said the son) of the Earl of Bath. His contempt for an upstart
tradesman is evident, but the effect of his piece, with the gratuitous
sneer in its last sentence, is likely to be the opposite of what was
intended, and his picture of the Newberys emerges as an endearing
one. I have shortened Colman's opening, which was a leisurely
setting of the scene.]

Thursday, July 7, 1763

Spectatum veniunt, veniunt spectentur ut —— OVID.

What is't, by coming here they mean?
They come to see, and to be seen.

THE reigning passion of this nation, for some few years past,
seems to have been the love of Shews, and Spectacles, and
Festivals, and Solemnities. During the war, the people
betrayed several symptoms of this rage after fine sights, and

many thousands followed the Camp, as young ensigns often take to the army, for the sake of its splendour and gaiety. One week all the vehicles in England from the coach and six, or landau with two postilions, down to the one-horse chaise and sober sulky, were whirling passengers along the road from all quarters towards Portsmouth, to see the Fleet assembled at Spithead; and the next, the same people were transported with the same rapidity, by the same passion for a sight and a crowd, to behold the evolutions and *manoeuvres* of the regiments of Militia embodied and encamped at Winchester. At the Coronation the tide of company from every county in the kingdom flowed, like rivers discharging themselves into the sea, into the metropolis. . . This summer, now that Oxford is become the scene wherein the Grand Shew is exhibited, and the doors of the Sheldonian Theatre are thrown open for almost a whole week, it is no wonder that London once more empties itself into this magnificent reservoir, and that all ranks and degrees of people are assembled to see the doctors in scarlet, and to attend the Lectures of TERRAE-FILIUS. There is not a man on earth, Ladies and Gentlemen, who is a truer lover of mirth and jollity than myself; and I take a most particular delight in the present ENCAENIA. It gives me an unspeakable pleasure to see the new *Dunstable-bonnets* mixt with square caps, and a gown and petticoat by the side of a gown and cassock. I could stand whole hours to see the white fustian riding-habits and blue sattin-waistcoats make their entry at East-Gate; and am transported to see the boot and the basket of all the stage-coaches filled with rosin and cat-gut, and fiddles, and hautboys, and clarionets, and french-horns, and bass-viols, while the inside and outside of every machine is crowded with the performers, English and Italian, vocal and instrumental. Festivals and Solemnities have, I grant, their uses and advantages; and far be it from me to attempt to erase any of the red-letter days from the *OXFORD*

ALMANACK! It must however at the same time be confessed that scenes of grandeur, and seasons of celebrity, which serve merely for relaxation to the studious, and fill the intelligent mind with great ideas, often prove only new occasions of idleness to the holy-day-making tradesmen, and open nothing but the mouth of the ignorant, who stand agape, gazing with a foolish face of pleasure and astonishment . . .

Going along the High-street last Tuesday morning I was observing, not without a smile, one of those modern tottering crazy vehicles, half-post-chaise, half-chariot, neither one nor the other, and yet something of both, driving towards the Angel Inn-yard; but turning my eyes from the carriage to the persons it contained, whom should I see but my good friend Mr FOLIO the bookseller, near St Paul's, and his wife, Mrs FOLIO; who at that very instant happening to dart the rays of her bright eyes in right angles upon me, she pulled my friend FOLIO by the sleeve, who seemed half asleep by her side.

FOLIO no sooner saw me than he ran his head and neck a yard and a half out of the chariot window, and bawled out lustily, "Mr ——!" — but hold, I must not tell my name. I followed the chariot into the Inn-yard, and had the honour of handing out Mrs FOLIO.

The first ceremonies occasioned by this our unexpected interview being over, and being quietly seated in the parlour, Mr FOLIO informed me, that having a new edition of a Jest-Book printing at a private press in Oxford, he took this opportunity of visiting the University and giving Mrs FOLIO an agreeable airing; after which he enquired very cordially after Mr Fletcher of the Turle, Mr Daniel Prince, and the rest of his brother booksellers in Oxford. I find too, continued he, you have a TERRAE-FILIUS — a new paper, I suppose — pray who is the Author? Does it make a noise? Does it sell? How many do they print? Would you be so kind now, my dear Sir (taking me by the hand and smiling) as to assist me in making proper extracts, and furnish me with a few occasional paragraphs to send up to the *Ledger*, and *Lloyd's Evening Post?* To these various interrogations I made no other reply, than enquiring after the younger part of the family, — I hope Miss FOLIO is well, Ma'am. — Very well, Sir, I thank you, said Mrs FOLIO; we had some thoughts of bringing her down with us, but my *spouse* had such a quantity of things to put into the chariot, that we could not easily crowd *three on us* into it: so I have left Polly in our lodgings at Islington Spa, and there, you know, she can't be [sunk?] for want of company, — and if she pleases, she may go to the *Wells* every night. — And how does young Mr FOLIO do? — What! *Bonus!* says Mr FOLIO, *Bonus* is entered in one of the colleges — He has left St Paul's School, and is a brother gownsman of yours; at which words he rang the bell, and on the appearance of the waiter, dispatched him to —— College for young Master FOLIO, desiring his company with some particular friends at the Angel.

Till the return of the messenger Mr FOLIO, after having dispatched another waiter to the barber's with his wig, amused himself with unpacking some parcels and valizes, which, it seems, were what had filled up Miss FOLIO's place in the chariot. The first he unfolded, he informed me, were some sheets of a new work of his own writing, which he proposed to publish early in the ensuing winter. He prest me very hard to read some particular passages, which I evaded, pleading want of time and leisure to give it due attention in the present hurry and dissipation of the place. — Come, come, says he, I know you gentlemen that write don't approve of *us in the trade* pretending to publish books of our own — but we have some *good hands* among us, I can tell you. — Oh, I know that. — Know it! Ay, but none of you care to own it. For anything courtly and airy, for a Dramatick Satire, or a modern Tragedy, we have Dodsley in Pall-Mall, — Mr Pope allowed *him* to be a good Poet — for Divinity and

Morality we have Payne that lives in the Row — for Criticism, or any thing in the *Belles Lettres* way, there is R. Griffiths, — why, he writes half the *Monthly Review* — and then for the whole *Circle of Sciences* there's our old friend Mr Newbery, at the North Door of St Paul's — and the Author of a late Pamphlet, called *The Lives of the present Writers*, assures us for a fact that he has wrote two favorite farces.

How much farther his zeal for the honour of *the Trade* would have carried him is uncertain, if his vehemence had not been broke in upon by the return of the messenger, and the arrival of Young FOLIO. The mother was charmed beyond expression with his appearance in the Academical Habit, and vowed he was grown half a head, or else that dress made him look so much taller. Well, I protest it becomes him vastly! Don't it? (turning to me). You must know, Sir, his father intends *making on him* a Clergyman. — Ay, ay, the gown by all means! said FOLIO. — But come, Bonus! you must shew your mother and me the University. Mr —— I hope will favour us with his company to make *the tower* of the Colleges, and return afterwards to eat a bit of mutton with us at dinner. I accepted the invitation, and Mr FOLIO having waited in his gold laced hat with a handkerchief of Mrs F's about his ears, till the return of his wig, properly bushed out and powdered, and having in the interim equipped himself with a full suit of pompadour with gold buttons, which he had brought down carefully packed between pasteboards, we sallied out of the Angel into the High-Street *to see the University.*

We were no sooner got into the street than we were carried by a kind of instinct into Mr Parker's, not only to give Mr FOLIO an opportunity of shaking his old friend by the hand, but also in order to furnish himself with one of Mr Prince's *Pocket Companion,* without which he declared it was impossible to go round the University. There, Sir, continued he, applying himself to me, there's another instance of *Genius* in a Bookseller. The *Pocket Companion* is all Mr PRINCE's *own*, — not only his own property, but his own writing. One of your gownsmen, indeed, has since wrote a *New Guide*, — but it won't do, — shaking his head, — it won't do, — much inferior to my Friend Daniel's.

We then crossed the way to Queen's College, where Bonus, as FOLIO called him, informed us that the East side of the square had been lately rebuilt, and that there had been some squabbles among the Fellows. FOLIO said the Chapel was fine, very fine, and quoted two lines out of Milton's *Spenseroso,* for so he termed it, about *a dim religious light.* As to Mrs FOLIO, she declared that nothing in the College pleased her so much as the figure over the door of *her Majesty in a Cage.* — But that, she said, was very pretty, and she liked it vastly.

We then proceeded to ALL SOULS and the RADCLIFFE LIBRARY, at the first of which places Bonus informed us that the Common Room there was remarkable for the best port in Oxford. Some of the Fellows, says he, have tost off four bottles of it a day for several years together, without doing them any manner of harm. FOLIO observed that neither the College Library nor the Radcliffe were as yet half sufficiently stocked, and it would be a rare job to have the furnishing of them with books. Mrs FOLIO said that the Radcliffe was a good deal like St Paul's, only not half so large or so handsome. A queer sort of building, Ma'am, said young Bonus — a mere pepper-box — and there (pointing to the turrets of All Souls) there are the sugar-casters. — This produced an universal laugh, which concluded with an exclamation of FOLIO's, — Well said, Bonus! egad, I don't think that would be amiss in the new edition of the Jokes.

We then entered the Schools' Quadrangle, where Mr FOLIO took upon himself to inform his wife that all the rudiments of learning were taught in that spot. Here, says he, my dear, (pointing) there are Lectures read every morning, — Here the

Students attend the Professor of Divinity, — and here they attend the History Professor — and here the Poetry Professor, — and here the Professor of Physick, — and here the Professor of Civil Law — and so on — all learned men that have large salaries on purpose to lecture their pupils in the sciences. — Ay, says Mrs FOLIO, it is no wonder that they have all so much *larning*. — It is impossible to recount half their observations on the Picture-Gallery, the Bodleian Library, the Arundel Marbles, the Pomfret Collection, the Clarendon Printing-House, the Theatre, and the Museum. I can only recollect that Mr FOLIO met with an acquaintance among the compositors at the printing-house, with whom he entered into conversation about the method of printing *Baskerville's* Bible without wetting the sheets before they were put to press; — and that he supposed a good deal of money might be made of the MSS in the Bodley; — that he compared the Museum to Don Saltero's Coffee-house, and that Mrs FOLIO at going-out asked the person who shew'd the room, *If there was no wax-work.* — In the rest of our circuit I remember nothing remarkable, except that Mrs FOLIO was extremely delighted with the Bason and Mercury in the centre of the great quadrangle at Christ-church, and told her husband she wished they had just such a one in the middle of their garden at Islington.

We then returned to the Angel, and as soon as dinner was ended and the cloth taken away, Well, Bonus, says FOLIO, and what hast thou learnt here? Tell us some of thy studies, — come, give your mother and me a *little touch* of the Mathematicks. — *Bonus,* being hard pressed, was obliged to comply; and drawing a kind of figure with his finger in the wine that was spilt on the table, uttered very gravely some incoherent jargon about A and B being equal to C and D, and parallel lines, and equilateral triangles. FOLIO and his wife observed him with infinite attention and the most visible delight; and as soon as he had done, This, says FOLIO, — this, my dear, (addressing himself to his wife) is what *we* call *Demonstration.* Sir, says Bonus, I did not think you had so good a notion of the Mathematicks. — Child, says Mrs FOLIO, your father has a general knowledge of every thing.

Not long after I took my leave, and could not help reflecting that to people like FOLIO and his wife, Sights and Shews afford but small entertainment and no instruction: and that it would be almost sufficient for the gratification of such minds if Grand Solemnities were to come round, like the year of Jubilee at Rome, or the blowing of the aloe, not above once in a hundred years.

MR NEWBERY'S LITTLE
BOOKS

Riddle-me-ree

from

FOOD *for the* MIND; *or,*
a New RIDDLE - BOOK

THERE was a thing a full month
    old,
  When *Adam* was no more ;
But 'ere that thing was five weeks old,
  Adam was years five score.

Mr Newbery's Little Books

THE LIST that follows is an attempt to single out the children's books from the rest of John Newbery's publishing output, and to give some impression of what they were like. My selection is based on Newbery's own advertisements of "books for the instruction and amusement of Little Masters and Misses." But it should not be seen as an attempt to set up a canon. Newbery's lists varied in length and content, presumably according to the space available and to what was currently in print; and sometimes, where the element of entertainment seems slight, it is hard to decide whether or not a title should be included. I have omitted most books that seem primarily instructional or educational, but have found space for the *Royal Primer*, the *New History of England* and *The Newtonian System of Philosophy* (which has a veneer of fiction, and is sometimes referred to as *Tom Telescope's Philosophy of Tops and Balls*.)

It can be argued that Newbery put his genius into his title-pages, which he used in shortened form for his advertisements. Some books are represented here by the full but most by the shorter form. They are arranged in their approximate order of publication, using Sydney Roscoe's bibliography as a guide; but the Newbery children's books are extremely rare, and some dates are still uncertain.

1744.   A LITTLE PRETTY POCKET-BOOK (see illustration, page 5.)

1750.   NURSE TRUELOVE'S CHRISTMAS-BOX: or, THE
        GOLDEN PLAYTHING FOR LITTLE CHILDREN: by
        which they may learn the Letters as soon as they can
        speak, and know how to behave so as to make every
        body love them. Adorned with Thirty Cuts. Price *One
        Penny*, bound and gilt.

1750?   NURSE TRUELOVE'S NEW-YEAR'S GIFT: or, THE
        BOOK OF BOOKS FOR CHILDREN. Embellished
        with Cuts, and designed for a Present to every little
        Boy who would become a great Man, and ride upon
        a fine Horse; and to every little Girl who would
        become a great Woman, and ride in a Lord-Mayor's
        gilt Coach. Price *Two-pence* bound and gilt.

1751.   THE LILLIPUTIAN MAGAZINE; or, THE YOUNG
        GENTLEMAN AND LADY'S GOLDEN LIBRARY, being
        an Attempt to mend the World, to render the Society
        of Man more amiable, and to establish the Plainness,
        Simplicity, Virtue and Wisdom of the Golden Age, so
        much celebrated by the Poets and Historians.
        Adorned with Copper-plate Cuts. Price *One Shilling*
        bound and gilt.

> Man in that Age no Rule but Reason knew,
> And with a native Bent did Good pursue:—
> Unforc'd by Punishment, unaw'd by Fear,
> His Words were simple and his Soul sincere.

1751.   The ROYAL PRIMER: Or, An easy and pleasant Guide
        to the Art of Reading. Interspersed with a great
        Variety of short and diverting Stories, with suitable
        Morals and Reflections. Adorned with 27 Cuts. Price
        Three-pence bound and gilt.

1752.   A PRETTY BOOK of *Pictures* for little Masters and
        Misses: Or, *Tommy Trip's* History of Birds and

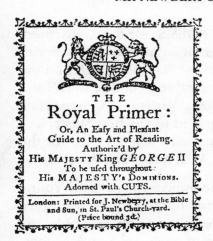

THE
Royal Primer:
Or, An Eafy and Pleafant
Guide to the Art of Reading.
Authoriz'd by
His MAJESTY King *GEORGE* II
To be ufed throughout:
His MAJESTY's DOMINIONS.
Adorned with.CUTS.

London: Printed for J. Newbery, at the Bible
and Sun, in St. Paul's Church-yard.
(Price bound 3d.)

A good Boy *and* Girl *at their Books.*

HE who ne'er learns his A, B, C,
For ever will a Blockhead be;
But he who to his book's inclin'd,
Will foon a golden treafure find.

Children like tender oziers take the bow,
And as they firft are fafhion'd always grow:
For what we learn in youth, to that alone,
In age we are by fecond nature prone.

Title and opening page from the *Royal Primer*

Beasts; with a familiar Description of each in Verse and Prose: To which is added, the History of little *Tom Trip* himself, of his Dog *Jouler,* and of *Woglog* the great Giant. Price *Six-pence* bound and gilt. (See illustration, page 136.)

1756.   THE LITTLE LOTTERY-BOOK for Children: Containing, a new Method of playing them into a Knowledge of the Letters, Figures, &c. Embellished with above 40 Cuts, and published with the Approbation of the Court of Common Sense. Price *Three-pence* bound and gilt.

1756.   A Collection of PRETTY POEMS, for the Amusement of Children three Foot high. By *Thomas Tagg,* Esq; Adorned with above Sixty Cuts. Price *6d* bound. [The "fifty-fourth edition" − dated 1756 and probably the first − was described on the title-page as "printed for the Booksellers of Europe, Asia, Africa and America and sold at the Bible and Sun in St Paul's Churchyard." By 1768 the "sixtieth edition" had been reached.]

1757. A collection of PRETTY POEMS, for the Amusement of Children six Foot high. Interspersed with a Series of Letters from Cousin SAM To Cousin SUE, on the Subjects of Criticism, Poetry, and Politics, with Notes *Variorum*. Adorned with a Variety of Copper-Plate Cuts, designed and engraved by the best Masters. . . Price *1s.* bound. [This title too was "Printed for the Booksellers of Europe, Asia, Africa and America."]

1757. FABLES IN VERSE for the Improvement of the Young and the Old. By *Abraham Aesop,* Esq; To which are added, FABLES in *Verse* and *Prose*, with the Conversation of Beasts at their several Meetings, Routs and Assemblies. By *Woglog* the Great Giant. Illustrated with a Variety of curious Cuts, and an Account of the Lives of the Authors. Price *6d* bound. [An edition of 1768, after Newbery's death, adds on its title-page, following "the Lives of the Authors," the words "by their old Friend Mr NEWBERY."]

1758. FOOD for the MIND: Or, A NEW RIDDLE BOOK: compiled for the Use of the great and the little good Boys and Girls of *England, Scotland,* and *Ireland.* By JOHN THE GIANT-KILLER, Esq; Adorned with Cuts. Price *Six-Pence* bound and gilt.

1758. BE MERRY and WISE: Or, The *Cream* of the *Jests* and *Marrow* of *Maxims,* for the Conduct of Life; published for the Use of all little good Boys and Girls, by *T. Trapwit, Esq;* Adorned with Cuts. Price 6d. bound and gilt. —— *Would you be agreeable in Company, and useful to Society, carry some merry Jests in your Mind, and honest Maxims in your Heart.* —— GROTIUS.

1759. A NEW HISTORY OF ENGLAND, from the Invasion of *Julius Caesar* to the Reign of King *George II.*

Adorned with Cuts of all the Kings and Queens who have reigned since the *Norman* Conquest. Price *Sixpence* bound and gilt. —— *The Memory of Things past ought not to be extinguished by Length of Time, nor great and admirable Actions remain destitute of Glory.* —— HERODOTUS.

1760.   A PRETTY PLAY-THING for Children of all Denominations: Containing, I. The Alphabet in Verse for the Use of little Children. II. An Alphabet in Prose, interspersed with proper Lessons in Life, for the Use of great Children. III. The Sound of the Letters explained by visible Objects. IV. The CUZ'S CHORUS, set to Music; to be sung by Children, in order to teach them to join their Letters into Syllables, and pronounce them properly. The whole

The Merry Philosopher.

Do you bite your Thumb at us, Sir?
Shakespeare.

Six-Pennyworth of WIT;

OR,

Little Stories for Little Folks,
Of all Denominations.

Adorned with CUTS.

Unhappy Wit, like most mistaken Things,
Atones not for the Envy which it brings.
So singeth that excellent Poet Master *Pope*; and therefore, when you have read this *Six-pennyworth of* WIT, you would do well to buy *Twelve-pennyworth of* WISDOM, which is much better, and may be had at the Place where this is sold. — *Wit* and *Wisdom* should always be blended together; for, as Mrs. *Margery Two-Shoes* observes, WIT *is* FOLLY, *unless a wise Man hath the keeping of it.*

LONDON:
Printed for CARNAN and NEWBERY, at Nº. 65, in St. Paul's Church-Yard; and sold by all the Booksellers in the World.
[Price Six-pence bound and gilt.]

Frontispiece and title-page from *Six-Pennyworth of Wit*, first published by John Newbery in 1767 embellished with Variety of Cuts, after the Manner of *Ptolomy*. Price *Three-pence* bound and gilt.

1761.   THE NEWTONIAN SYSTEM OF PHILOSOPHY Adapted to the Capacities of young GENTLEMEN and LADIES, and familiarized and made entertaining by Objects with which they are intimately acquainted: being the Substance of SIX LECTURES read to the LILLIPUTIAN SOCIETY, By TOM TELESCOPE, A.M., And collected and methodized for the Benefit of the Youth of these Kingdoms, by their old Friend, Mr NEWBERY, in *St. Paul's Church Yard*; Who has also added Variety of Copper-Plate Cuts, to illustrate and confirm the Doctrines advanced. (See illustrations, pages 10 and 11.)

1765.   The Renowned History of GILES GINGERBREAD; a little Boy who lived upon Learning. Price *One Penny* bound, gilt, and adorned with Cuts.

> See, here's little *Giles*
>   With his Gingerbread Book,
> For which he doth long,
>   And at which he doth look;
> Till by longing and looking
>   He gets it by Heart,
> And then eats it up
>   As we eat up a Tart.
>
>   —*TOM TAGG.*

1765.   The EASTER-GIFT: Or, the Way to be very good.—*A Book very much wanted*. Price *Two-pence* bound, gilt, and adorned with Cuts.

1765.   The WHITSUNTIDE GIFT: Or, the Way to be very happy—*A Book necessary for all Families*. Price *Two-pence* bound, gilt, and embellished with Cuts.

1765.   The VALENTINE'S-GIFT: Or, the whole History of

THE
HISTORY
OF
Little GOODY TWO-SHOES;
Otherwife called,
Mrs. MARGERY TWO-SHOES.
WITH
The Means by which fhe acquired her
Learning and Wifdom, and in confe-
quence thereof her Eftate; fet forth
at large for the Benefit of thofe,

Who from a State of Rags and Care,
And having Shoes but half a Pair;
Their Fortune and their Fame would fix,
And gallop in a Coach and Six.

See the Original Manufcript in the *Vatican*
at *Rome,* and the Cuts by *Michael Angelo.*
Illuftrated with the Comments of our
great modern Critics.

The THIRD EDITION.

LONDON:
Printed for J. NEWBERY, at the *Bible* and
Sun in St. *Paul's-Church-Yard,* 1766.
[Price Six-pence.]

Little Goody Two-Shoes.

Frontispiece and title-page of *Little Goody Two-Shoes,* from the third
edition, dated 1766. The first edition, dated 1765, of which
there is a copy in the British Library, is virtually identical

Valentine's-Day: Containing the Way to preserve
Truth, Honour, and *Integrity* unshaken.—— *Very*
necessary in a trading Nation. Price *6d* bound, gilt,
and embellished with Cuts.

1765.   The Renowned History of Little GOODY TWO-
SHOES. . . Price *Six-pence* bound, gilt, and embellished with Cuts. (See illustration above.)

1765.   The FAIRING: Or, Golden Toy for Children,

In which they may see all the Fun of the Fair
And at Home be as happy as if they were there.

A Book of great Consequence to all whom it may
concern. Price *Six-pence* bound, gilt, and adorned
with Cuts.

1767.   Six-Pennyworth of WIT; Or, Little Stories for Little Folks, Of all Denominations. Adorned with CUTS . . . Printed for J.NEWBERY. . . and sold by all the Booksellers in the World. Price *Six-pence* bound and gilt. (See illustration on page 131.)

1767.   TOM THUMB'S FOLIO; Or, a new penny Plaything for little Giants, to which is prefixed an Abstract of the Life of Mr Thumb and an historical account of the wonderful Deeds he performed, together with some Anecdotes respecting Grumbo the Great Giant. Printed for the People of all Nations. Price *One Penny*.

1767.   THE TWELFTH-DAY GIFT; Or, THE GRAND EXHIBITION, containing a curious Collection of Pieces in Prose and Verse (many of them originals) which were delivered to a numerous and polite Audience, on the important subjects of Religion &c. &c. Price *1s.* bound and gilt.

TO THE

TRUE and GENUINE

LOVERS of NOISE,

This BOOK,

Which was calculated for their Amusement, and written for their Use,

Is most humbly inscribed

By

YOU KNOW WHO.

✦✦✦✦✦✦✦✦:✦✦✦✦✦✦

THE

FAIRING.

CHAP. I.

Which begins in a Manner not prescribed by the Ancients.

HALLO Boys, hallo Boys.—— *Huzza! Huzza! Huzza!*

Come *Tom*, make Haste, for the Fair is begun. See, here is *Jack Pudding* with the Gridiron on his Back, and all the Boys hallooing.

Dedication and opening page from *The Fairing*
(not facing pages in original)

TOMMY TRIP AND HIS
DOG JOULER

Woglog the Great Giant: left, from a copperplate engraving in the *Lilliputian Magazine*; right, in an adapted and softened version, from *A Pretty Book of Pictures*

Tommy Trip and his Dog Jouler

JOHN NEWBERY created, or at any rate sponsored, an array of imaginary authors and characters with memorable names. Nurse Truelove, Tom Telescope, T. Trapwit, Tom Tagg and Tommy Trip (the initial T was obviously a favourite) jostle with Giles Gingerbread, Goody Two-Shoes and Woglog the Great Giant. Some of them, having made their first appearance, recur in later titles. Even the Little Master Tommy and Pretty Miss Polly for whose instruction and amusement the *Little Pretty Pocket-Book* was devised may be spotted some years later making a discreet appearance in the *Pretty Book of Pictures*, now grown up and doing credit to their upbringing:

> See how this pretty well-bred Pair
> Together ride to take the Air,
> While harmless Chat, of various Kinds,
> Enlivens and improves their Minds.

Master Tommy and Miss Polly, "the promising Youth and the beautiful Fair," also dance a graceful minuet, to the delight of their proud parents.

The deeds of the Newbery characters were usually less inspiring, to modern minds, than their names. The moral and cautionary aspects of their stories were always prominent. I have chosen the story of Tommy Trip, his dog Jouler and Woglog the great Giant for reprinting here: not for any great literary merit but because Goldsmith's account of the "philanthropic bookseller in St Paul's Churchyard" said that he was "at that time actually compiling materials for the history of one Mr Thomas Trip." This is the flimsiest of evidence for authorship by Newbery, especially as Goldsmith himself was speaking in the person of a fictional character, but it is hard to find better. Apart from such figures as Tagg and Trapwit, the Newbery children's books have no apparent authors.

The story appeared in the *Lilliputian Magazine* in 1751 and was reprinted in *A Pretty Book of Pictures* in 1752. What follows is the later version.

> Tommy TRIP, the Author of the following Sheets, is the only Son of Mr William Trip of Spittle-fields, London. He is but short in Stature, not much bigger than *Tom Thumb,* but a great deal better; for he is a good Scholar, and whenever you see him, you will always find him with a Book in his Hand, and his faithful Dog *Jouler* by his side. *Jouler* serves him for a Horse as well as a Dog, and *Tommy,* when he has a mind to ride, pulls a little bridle out of his pocket, whips it upon honest *Jouler,* and away he gallops, tantwivy. As he rides thro' the Town, he frequently stops at the Doors, to know how the little Children do within, and if they are good and learn their Books? and then leaves an Apple, an Orange, or a Plumb-cake at the Door, and away he gallops again, tantwivy, tantwivy, tantwivy.

> You have heard how he beat *Woglog* the great Giant, I suppose, Have you not? But lest you should not, I will tell you:— As *Tommy* was walking through a Meadow on a moon-light Night, he heard a little Boy cry, upon which he called to *Jouler,* bridled him, and galloped away to the Place; when he came there, he found *Woglog* with a little Boy under his Arm, whom he was going to throw into the Water. Little Boys should never loiter about in the Fields, nor even in the Streets after it is dark. However, as he had been a good Boy in other Respects, little *Trip* was determined the Giant should not hurt him; and therefore he called to him. "Here you great Giant, you *Woglog!* set

down the little Boy, or I'll make you dance like a Pea on a Tobacco-Pipe! Are not you ashamed to set your Wit to a Child?" *Woglog* turned round, attempted to seize little *Trip* between his Finger and Thumb, and thought to have cracked him as one does a Walnut; but just as his Hand came to him, *Jouler* snapped at it, and bit a piece of his Thumb, which put the Giant in so much Pain, that he let fall the little Boy, who ran away. Little *Trip* then up with his Whip and lashed *Woglog* till he lay down, and roared like a town Bull, and promised never to meddle with any little Boys and Girls again. After he had thus beat the Giant, *Trip* put the little Boy upon *Jouler*, and carried him home to his Father and Mother; but upon the Road he charged him to be a good Boy, and to say his Prayers, and learn his Book, and do as his Papa and Mamma bid him, which this little Boy has done ever since; and so must all other little Boys and Girls, or no body will love them.

Here, in the *Lilliputian Magazine*, the story ends, but in the *Pretty Book of Pictures* it continues, somewhat inconsequently:

Little *Trip* is not only a very agreeable Companion, and a great Scholar, but is also allowed to be one of the best Poets of the Age, and that even by the Poets themselves, which, in my Opinion, is an incontestable Proof of his superior Abilities; For if he did not as much exceed those Gentry as Apollo does the Muses, they, who seldom make Confessions of this Sort, would never give up the Point in his Favour. He has now by him several Dramatic Pieces, which are not culled from other Authors, as the Custom is, but all Originals, and well adapted to the English Stage; and the following Song compos'd by him, when he was very young, will sufficiently prove his Superiority in Lyric Poetry.

Three Children sliding on the Ice
Upon a Summer's Day;
As it fell out they all fell in,
The rest they ran away.

Now had these Children been at School
Or sliding on dry Ground,
Ten thousand Pounds to one Penny
They had not all been drown'd.

You parents who have Children dear
And eke you that have none,
If you would keep them safe Abroad,
Pray keep them all at Home.

The attribution of this familiar bit of nonsense to Tommy
Trip is itself a bit of nonsense. The Opies' *Oxford Dictionary
of Nursery Rhymes* places it in the seventeenth century and
quotes the word of a publisher in 1680 that it was a "choice
Peice of Drollery" which was "Got by Heart and often
repeated by divers witty Gentlemen and Ladies that used to
walk in the *New Exchange,* and at their Recreations in *Hide
Park.*" It is odd that it should be placed here, since it
appears to satirize the children-should-be-safe-at-home
message of the story that precedes it.

In the *Fables in Verse* by Abraham Aesop Esq. (1757), to
which Woglog the Great Giant contributes some additions,
Woglog has become a reformed character who "employed
his Time chiefly in relieving those who were in Distress, and
correcting those who were turbulent and unruly." His
methods of persuasion can be drastic but effective. "He once
met with nine Gentlemen going into a Gaming-house near St
James's, whom he swung heavily over his head, and so
frightened them that they returned home to their Families,
said their Prayers, went to Bed, and determined ever after to
leave off their knavish, stupid, unChristian, immoral,
inhuman, vile, wicked, scandalous Practice." The reformed
Woglog also does his bit for his sponsor, for while in Bath
he "stept into Mr *Leake's*" — a bookstore — "to read one of
Mr *Newbery's* little Books."

SIDELIGHTS

John Rowe Townsend

EARLIER NEWBERYS
THE *READING MERCURY*
THE NEWBERY BOOKS IN AMERICA
THE INHERITORS

Riddle-me-ree

from

FOOD *for the* MIND; *or,*
a New RIDDLE-BOOK

'TIS true I have both face and
hands,
And move before your eye ;
Yet when I go my body stands,
And when I stand I lie.

Sidelights

1. *Earlier Newberys*

BY THE TIME John Newbery was born in 1713 at Waltham St Lawrence, on the fringe of the great Windsor forest, the Newbery family had long been established as yeomen farmers in Berkshire and other counties of England's South and West. The births, marriages and deaths of numerous Newberys are recorded in the parish registers at Waltham from the beginning of the reign of Queen Elizabeth I onwards. (The short form Waltham will be used here for brevity, and the subject of this book will be referred to as JN, partly to distinguish him from other John Newberys.) JN was the son of a small farmer, and his elder brother Robert remained in Waltham as a farmer; to judge from his letter quoted on page 54, Robert was only just literate. Yet, as Charles Welsh says, there were family connections with the book trade.

Welsh, citing (in 1885) "a pedigree in possession of the present family," says that JN's descent can be traced from Ralph Newbery (1535-1606), who was a leading figure in Elizabethan publishing and printing and published many of the most important books of his day. Family historians are sometimes tempted to leap across gaps, and the scrupulous researches of Mr Ronald Newbery in the present generation have not as yet confirmed this descent. However, Ralph

Newbery was born and died in Waltham, purchased a manor there on his retirement, and endowed the Newbery charity there.

Mr Ronald Newbery traces with fair probability the descent of JN, through three generations of Robert Newberys, from an earlier John Newbery who married Margaret Dormar at Waltham in 1627. This John was entered in the parish register as Johannes. A "Johanes Newbery," son of Ralph Newbery, was baptized at Waltham in 1590, and it seems possible that this was the same John. But, as Mr Ronald Newbery has remarked, John Newberys were plentiful at the time. Whether or not there is a direct line of descent from Ralph the publisher and printer, it is beyond reasonable doubt that he and JN were related.

Ralph was not the only Newbery to be active in the Elizabethan book world. The late Edmund Newbery, who ran the Newbery Press in Clapham, London, published in 1960 a little book called *The Newberys,* in which he identified one Thomas Newbery (*floruit* 1563) as Ralph's elder brother. Thomas was the author of the *Booke in Englyssh metre of the great marchaunt man called Dyves Pragmaticus, very pretye for chyldren to rede.* This has some claim to be considered the first set of verses specifically written for children, as distinct from the long oral tradition of song, rhyme and ballad. It was designed to help children "rede and write Wares and Implements in this worlde contayned," and in spite of its utilitarian purpose it is rather engaging:

> I have Suchet, Sirrup, greene Ginger and Marmalade,
> Biscuit, Cumfect and Carraways as fine as can be made,
> As for Potecary and Grocery, I have all that trade.
> You shall se of all thyngs, come hether to me.

> I have here to sell fine Needells and Thimbles,
> Nayle pearsers, smalle podde Chyselles and Wimbels,
> Blades, and for weavers fine Shuttells and Brembils.
> What do you lacke, friend? Come hether to me.

I have inkyll, Crewell, and gay Valances fine,
Pannes to warm Bedde, with girte corde and lyne.
The money is your owne and the ware is myne,
Come see for your love, and come bye of me.

As I observed in my study of children's literature *Written
for Children,* "the evocative names of the wares and the
unmistakable tones of the salesman make the verses still
pleasing, if not exactly literature."

However, the identification of this Thomas Newbery as
Ralph's brother must be looked on with caution; if Edmund
Newbery had evidence he did not set it out in his book, and
very little of his work on the family history has survived.

Even more speculative, in the absence of other evidence,
is Edmund Newbery's statement that Ralph was the nephew
of John Newbery, an Elizabethan merchant whom the
historian Sir William Foster in his book on *England's Quest
of Eastern Trade* called "as intrepid an adventurer as
England ever bred." This John Newbery, after two eventful
voyages to the Near East and Persia, set out in 1583 at the
head of a trading mission, armed with letters of introduction
from Queen Elizabeth I to the Mogul emperor of India and
the "King of China." After surviving various perils and being
imprisoned by the Portuguese, Newbery and two companions reached India and appear to have got to the emperor's
court; but Newbery, returning alone to report on his
experiences and arrange a further venture, disappeared on
the way back. No one knows what became of him.

The only certain link of this John Newbery with Ralph,
other than that they had the same surname, is that John was
the "assured good friend" of Richard Hakluyt, and that Ralph
was joint publisher of Hakluyt's *Voyages,* which included
several letters sent by Newbery in the course of his travels.
An undoubted line of association can be drawn from
Newbery the merchant adventurer through Hakluyt, Ralph
the publisher, and the Newberys of Waltham St Lawrence to

Newbery the bookseller, but it does not seem safe to claim more than that.

Interestingly, however, the earlier and the later Newbery shared an unremitting devotion to trade. The merchant adventurer's letters, as printed by Hakluyt, are rarely about glories seen or strange customs witnessed; they are concerned with the prices and demand for goods, and the bribes and duties that had to be paid. Cecil Tragen, who told the story of the travels of Newbery and his associate Ralph Fitch in a book called *Elizabethan Venture*, published in London in 1953, remarked that the diary of his travels might well have been titled "Newbery's Eastern Market Guide (Persia and Turkey.)" These two Newberys, if not kin, were obviously kindred spirits.

Edmund Newbery, in his little book, remarked on the number of Newberys over the years who had "left the plough for the press" and gone into the book trade. He named eighteen, including JN, his son and nephew, and his nephew's widow. Among the earlier ones was a John Newbery who traded from the Ball, in St Paul's Churchyard, from 1594 to 1603. According to Edmund, he was the son of John Newbery the explorer, but in the absence of confirmatory evidence it must seem more likely that he was the John Newbery of Waltham who was apprenticed to Ralph in 1578. There were also two Nathaniel Newberys who traded from 1616 to 1634 and 1634 to 1653 respectively, Thomas Newbery who was a printer and publisher from 1653 to 1656, and William Newbery, a publisher from 1685 to 1701. None of these can with certainty be linked to JN; nor can Humphrey Newbery, the Utter Barrister of Lincoln's Inn, referred to by Welsh, although as Humphrey was buried at Waltham he may be presumed to be a kinsman. (Utter barristers in his day were those who were privileged, on account of their "learning and continuance," to practise as advocates in the higher courts of law.)

The Newbery charity was set up in 1608 by Ralph Newbery's son Francis in fulfilment of his father's wish to assure "to the use and relief of the poor inhabitants of Lawrence Waltham" a dwelling-house and piece of land in the parish. The Bell Inn, a fine old building with overhanging upper storeys and timber beams, stands on the land and still provides funds from which the trustees make donations to needy inhabitants of the parish. Visitors are told — in a punning reference to the Bell's situation — that it "sells beer by the Pound."

2. The "Reading Mercury"

The *Mercury,* John Newbery's starting point in publishing and printing, was one of the oldest and most respected of British local newspapers, founded in 1723. It ran, with occasional variations of title, for more than 250 years. Newbery joined it in its early days, and by the time he was 26, at the end of 1739, he was in control. Four years later he left Reading for the wider horizons of London, but he retained an interest in the *Mercury* throughout his life. Another nineteen years on — five years before he died — he put his stepdaughter Anna Maria Smart, formerly Carnan, in charge, with his stepson John Carnan as printer; and when Anna Maria died the paper passed into the control of the Cowslade family, into which her daughter had married.

It is clear from the paper's early files that Welsh's account is inaccurate. The *Mercury* was started on July 8, 1723, not, as Welsh suggests, by John Watts, a leading citizen of Reading, but by two printers, W. Parks and D. Kinnier. Parks went to America the following year; Kinnier continued, but by 1727 had been succeeded by William Ayres. It was to Ayres that John Newbery "engaged himself" in 1730. (He was said, according to an article in the 250th anniversary number of the paper, which was now the *Berkshire Mercury*, to have walked the ten miles from Waltham St Lawrence to Reading to make the acquaintance of Ayres, who thereupon took him on.)

By February 1737 the publisher of *The Reading Mercury or London Spy* was William Carnan. Carnan died at the end of that year, leaving his personal estate to his brother Charles, a linen-draper in Reading, and John Newbery. The imprint in 1738 was that of Mary Carnan (Carnan's widow, whom Newbery married). In July 1739 it was John Carnan and Company, and in November 1739 John Carnan for John Newbery. In 1741 the paper was "Printed by J. Newbery and C. Micklewright, at the Bible and Crown in the Market Place. Where ADVERTISEMENTS are taken in, if small, at 2s 6d each. And PRINTING, in general, is perform'd in the Neatest Manner." But the business extended far beyond printing, for an advertisement in the *Mercury's* columns on September 29, 1740, announced that

> John Newbery at the *Bible and Crown* in the Market Place, Reading, keeps a wholesale warehouse, and furnishes shopkeepers with all sorts of haberdashery goods (such as threads, tapes, bindings, ribbons, pins, needles etc.) as cheap as in London. And any person by sending a letter to him will be as well served as if they came in person.

Clearly Newbery would sell anything that would make a profit. The issue of October 26, 1741, had an advertisement for

the famous new-invented
BLACKING BALL FOR SHOES

which by experience of thousands has been found to be the best that was ever invented for that Purpose. It gives the Shoes a fine Gloss, black as Jet, and has these excellent properties: That it will not in the least daub or soil the Fingers in putting on the Shoe, or the Stockings in wearing, and is an excellent Preservative against the Wet, making the Shoe thereby wear a considerable Time longer. . . These

Balls are sold by John Newbery at the Bible and Crown in the Market Place, Reading.

The sale of patent medicines was already established. There was a large advertisement for Daffy's *Elixir Salutis,* "appointed to be sold at the Warehouse kept by John Newbery at the Bible and Crown in the Market Place at Reading, Berks, where all Shopkeepers in the South and West of England are invited to apply for the same, and they may depend upon having that which is genuine, with a good Allowance for their Trouble in selling it again."

The elixir was "one of the choicest Remedies for the following Disorders and Distempers, viz. Coughs, Colds, Asthmas and Phthisick, Agues, Cholick and Griping of the Guts, Consumption and bad Digestion, Distempers in Children, Dropsy, Eviscerations in the Kidneys and Bladder, Gout and Rheumatism, Green Sickness, Piles, Spleen, Fits of the Mother [hysteria], Vapours, Scurvy, Gravel in the Kidneys, Stone in the Bladder, etc."

Newbery was already interested in publishing, as the schemes noted in his 1740 tour indicate, and in that year he brought out, with Micklewright, *The Whole Duty of Man,* a reprint of a seventeenth-century didactic work, and *Miscellaneous Works for the Amusement of the Fair Sex.* Whether Micklewright was partner, employee or business associate is not clear, but Newbery was obviously the moving spirit. In 1743 Newbery moved to London; John Carnan and Micklewright stayed in Reading, where John Carnan remained as a printer until his death in 1785. A few years earlier the London printer William Bowyer had employed a C. Micklewright as compositor and later as overseer; most likely this was the same man. In December 1744 Bowyer printed for Newbery and Micklewright two thousand copies of *A True Account of a Voyage to the South Seas,* by Thomas Pascoe.

In 1745 the *Mercury's* imprint was "C. Micklewright & Co." Micklewright died in 1755 and his daughter Mary took over; she married one Charles Pocock (who added wall-paper to the goods sold from the Reading address.) In 1762, Newbery set up Anna Maria — effectively widowed by the collapse of her marriage to Christopher Smart — in control of the business, which he appears to have retrieved from Pocock.

Anna Maria ran the firm successfully for many years in the style of Anna Maria Smart and Company, and lived to the age of 77, dying in 1811. She enjoyed for many years (as her obituary notice in the *Mercury* said) a fine state of health. "A Catholic in religion, a Christian in the spirit of the Character, she never enquired the principles of anyone who solicited her help." Her elder daughter Marianne had married Thomas Cowslade in 1784, and after Anna Maria's death the paper was in the hands of the Cowslade family for more than a hundred years. It ceased publication in 1987.

3. *The Newbery books in America*

Old tales and rhymes, needing no cargo space but people's heads, crossed the ocean like stowaways with the early settlers in the American colonies. There they could survive without paper to print on or the sanction of spiritual leaders through the years of Puritan ascendancy, when the approved books for children were works of instruction and indoctrination, designed above all to save young souls from hellfire. Many of the latter, such as the famous *Token for Children,* by James Janeway, "being an exact Account of the Conversion, holy and exemplary Lives, and joyful Deaths of several young Children," were originally imports from England, afterwards printed in the colonies with American additions. Many were threats and exhortations from solemn and forbidding divines. But the disreputable old stuff still raised its unregenerate head, and Cotton Mather complained in 1713 of "foolish Songs and Ballads, which Hawkers and Peddlars carry into all Parts of the Countrey." He urged as an antidote "poetical Compositions full of Piety," such as "the excellent Watts's hymns."[1]

The excellent Dr Isaac Watts's *Divine Songs,* themselves an import from England, and milder than most hellfire preaching though still drawing attention to the "everlasting pains" that awaited sinners, became immensely popular in colonial America, and were continually reprinted there. But the great American work for children was the *New England Primer,* estimated to have sold between six and eight million copies between 1680 and 1830. (Even this may have had English origins.) It was intended to teach children to read — that is, to read the Bible — and combined the ABC with the elements of Puritan religious instruction.

The *Royal Primer,* apparently the first Newbery publication to be reprinted in America, offered what Cornelia Meigs called "wholesome competition" to the "stiff-necked" New England compilation.[2] It was published — described as being "improved" — by one James Chattin in Philadelphia in 1753, and the title-page claimed, in the same terms as the Newbery edition, that it was "an easy and pleasant Guide to the Art of Reading." The contents included a good deal of pious matter but were nevertheless much lighter than those of the *New England Primer,* with more entertainment and a notable shortage of hell fire. There were other American printings of the *Royal Primer,* play being made with the book's authorization "by His Majesty King George II. To be used throughout His Majesty's Dominions."

The large-scale reprinting of Newbery titles however had to wait for the American Revolution. Before this, English

---

[1] Quoted by A.S.W. Rosenbach, introduction to *Early American Children's Books,* p. xl.

[2] Cornelia Meigs, *A Critical History of Children's Literature,* p.117.

children's books were undoubtedly imported, but it is impossible to say which titles and in what numbers. Newbery's *Fables in Verse,* by "Abraham Aesop, Esq.," with assistance from Woglog the Great Giant, made an appearance in America in 1762, and the *Lilliputian Magazine* (1751) carried a list of young subscribers which included a contingent of fifty from various addresses in Maryland. In 1775 Hugh Gaine of New York introduced *Little Goody Two-Shoes.* But the American name especially associated with Newbery is that of Isaiah Thomas of Worcester, Massachusetts (1749-1831), who has been described as "the most important American printer and publisher of his generation."[1]

During the Revolutionary War, Thomas, a noted patriot, spirited his press out of Boston by water from under the noses of the British, and used it to defy them in print; but his patriotism did not inhibit him from importing and selling a stock of the Newbery children's books. After the war, when it was difficult for Americans to import from England, he began to print Newbery books on his own presses. American printers were then free, as Clifford Shipton wrote, "to reprint any English work which they saw fit without even a thank-you to the author." Copyright as between the two countries did not exist, and Thomas did not find it necessary to pay anything to Newbery's successors. (Newbery himself had died in 1767.)

Among Thomas editions I have seen are *Nurse Truelove's Christmas Box* and *Nurse Truelove's New Year's Gift* (1786), *Be Merry and Wise* (1786), *A Little Pretty Pocket-Book* (1787) and *Little Goody Twoshoes* ("Twoshoes" as one word, 1787.) Thomas changed the Newbery title-pages to read, "THE FIRST WORCESTER EDITION: Printed at Worcester,

---

[1] Clifford K. Shipton, in *Isaiah Thomas: Printer, Patriot, and Philanthropist.*

Massachusetts, by Isaiah Thomas, and SOLD, Wholesale and Retail, at his Book-Store." He also made sporadic attempts to adapt the books to an American readership. *Nurse Truelove's New Year's Gift* is said on the title-page of the British edition to be designed as "a present to. . . every little Girl who would become a fine Woman, and ride in a Lord Mayor's gilt Coach;" in Thomas's edition this has become "a Governour's gilt Coach." In the *Little Pretty Pocket-Book* the "Britons" who "fly over the Main" in "The little k Play" have become sailors of unspecified nationality; *Little Goody Twoshoes* is inscribed to "young Gentlemen and Ladies who are good or intend to be good" not by "their old Friend in St Paul's Church-Yard" but by "their old Friend in Worcester." Thomas did not have modern means of producing facsimiles, and the type was reset page by page, to make the pagination and space available for illustrations the same as in the originals; the drawings were likewise recut but based on the originals.

Isaiah Thomas also reprinted works published by Newbery's imitators and successors. His appropriations have been looked on by some with disapproval, but at least they benefited his young readers, and Shipton remarked that "if the roll of [his] good works was consulted in relation to his admission to the pearly gates, there is no doubt that his children's books carried more weight than his Bibles." Other printers in Boston, New York and Philadelphia helped themselves to British publications in a similar way; and the practice continued into the next generation, when the work of such writers as Ann and Jane Taylor, Hannah More, Anna Letitia Barbauld and Mary Martha Sherwood was freely drawn upon. But British publishers were to get their own back before long, with wholesale piracies and imper-sonations of Peter Parley, otherwise known as Samuel G. Goodrich.

One hundred and fifty-five years after John Newbery's

death, Frederic Melcher — an innovative bookseller who became editor of *Publishers Weekly* and devoted much of his life to the enthusiastic promotion of good books for children — proposed at the conference of the American Library Association that a medal should be awarded each year by the A.L.A. for the most distinguished American children's book. Mr Melcher's proposal was adopted, his offer to present such a medal was accepted, and the title chosen was the John Newbery Medal. The award — still the most prestigious in the children's book world — has been made annually since 1922. John Newbery never heard of the United States of America, but, thanks to Mr Melcher and the A.L.A., millions of Americans have heard of him.

4. The inheritors

John Newbery was eminently a family man. He looked after both sides of his family — Carnans and Newberys — and did his best to keep the family together. But Francis Newbery, his only son, was the favoured member; it was Francis the son who was sent to Oxford and Cambridge and to whom the patent medicine business was left outright. Thomas Carnan, the stepson, and Francis Newbery, the nephew, went, like Newbery himself, into the bookselling and publishing trade, while the other stepson, John Carnan, remained a printer in Reading.

In his will, Newbery left the bookselling business to be carried on jointly by Francis the son, Francis the nephew and Thomas Carnan; but this did not happen. Francis the nephew had opened a business of his own during John Newbery's lifetime, at 15 Paternoster Row. According to Elizabeth Le Noir de la Brosse, who was the daughter of Anna Maria Smart and niece of Thomas Carnan, this Francis had been apprenticed to John Newbery, and it was JN who established

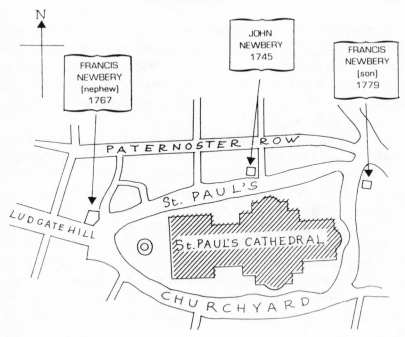

The premises in St Paul's Churchyard of John Newbery, his son, and
his nephew, with the years in which they entered into occupation

him in Paternoster Row. He was "doing very well in a snug
way," wrote Mrs Le Noir, until "a dashing shop on the
Ludgate Hill corner roused his ambition to a rivalry with his
uncle and benefactor."[1] Mrs Le Noir was of the other faction
and may not have been an impartial witness. Whether or not
a rift had already occurred, it was clearly John Newbery's
dying wish to unite the threesome. He failed, and Francis
the nephew, in his "dashing shop" at the corner of St Paul's
Churchyard, was soon in fierce competition with the other
two. Their resentment of him is made clear in title-pages and
advertisements cited by Welsh; they continued in the old

---

[1] Letter from Mrs Le Noir to E.H. Barker dated April 14, 1830, quoted by
Roscoe.

premises and held on grimly to the John Newbery titles, maintaining with some justice that they were the actual successors. Francis the nephew, unable to print his uncle's titles, was more productive and innovative as a publisher of children's books than the rival firm; neither of them, however, had the John Newbery touch.

The partnership of Carnan and Newbery the son lasted for twelve years but seems itself to have been an uneasy one. Carnan was a cantankerous fellow who did most of the work and no doubt resented it, while Newbery was self-important and had another business to attend to. The style of the firm varied, being usually "Newbery and Carnan" in the early years and "Carnan and Newbery" later. In 1779 Newbery transferred his home and the medicine business to a new building at the north-east corner of the churchyard; Carnan continued the bookselling arm at the old address, Number 65, and from 1782 published under his own name only. He died a bachelor in 1788. Francis Power, the son of Newbery's daughter Mary, published a few books from the old address, emphasizing that he was the founder's grandson; but in 1792 or 1793 he gave up and the original Newbery business came to an end.

Over at the corner, Francis Newbery the nephew had died (in 1780), but the firm he began was still flourishing in the hands of his widow Elizabeth, helped by a capable manager, Abraham Badcock, who may well have been in effective charge.

Elizabeth Newbery retired in 1802, having issued a large number of books — many of them tediously pious and didactic — and the business was taken over by her then manager, John Harris (1756-1846). Harris had much of John Newbery's innovative energy. He is best remembered as publisher of William Roscoe's *The Butterfly's Ball*, with illustrations by William Mulready, and its string of successors: *The Lion's Masquerade, The Elephant's Ball,* and

The Peacock "At Home." According to the *Dictionary of National Biography* he "amassed an ample fortune." His son, John Harris II, followed him.

The post-Harris history of the firm is outlined in the second appendix to the 1982 edition of Darton's *Children's Books in England,* on which I have drawn for the summary that follows. In 1843 the firm was taken over by E.C. Grant and W.D. Griffith and became Grant and Griffith. In 1856 Griffith took Robert Farran as partner and they traded for many years as Griffith and Farran, later Griffith, Farran and Company. Griffith died in 1877; in the 1880s Farran was joined by one H.J.P.Okeden and by Charles Welsh, John Newbery's biographer, the firm becoming briefly Griffith, Farran, Okeden and Welsh.

At the end of the decade Farran died and the firm closed down the bookshop in St Paul's Churchyard, where it and its predecessors had been continuously in business for well over a century. It continued publishing from Newbery House, 39 Charing Cross Road, and from 1889 to 1894 issued the monthly *Newbery House Magazine,* to which Welsh contributed articles on John Newbery and on children's books. He left about the end of 1891, and the firm's title reverted to Griffith, Farran & Co. The heart seems to have gone out of it, and from now on it declined. In 1897 a Mr Browne took control and it became Griffith, Farran, Browne & Co.; a few years later it went back once more to the old name of Griffith, Farran. It moved several times before ending its days in 1911 or 1912 almost where its founder, Francis Newbery the nephew, had begun, at 16-17 Paternoster Row.

◇

The patent medicine business, which passed from John Newbery to Francis the son, had an even longer life. The Oxford-educated Francis ran it after his father died, and defended Dr James's Powder at length and with great intensity at the time of the Goldsmith disaster; but although he was and remained "in trade" his ambition clearly was to become a country gentleman. His interests lay largely outside his business: he was passionately devoted to the violin (which, in spite of Johnson's remark, he seems to have played well), and at school and Oxford he "spent much time in private theatricals, to the detriment of his studies."[1] He was said also to be an ardent sportsman, and in 1791 he purchased the estate of Lord Heathfield in Sussex, afterwards becoming High Sheriff of the county.

Though not quite a poet, Francis Newbery was a competent versifier. In 1770 he had married Mary Raikes, sister of Robert Raikes the philanthropist and founder of Sunday Schools; and years later he celebrated this event in lines which appeared in a slim, privately printed volume called *Donum Amicis* (1815). The verses, described by him as "written in the year 1803, when the author was threescore," tell how his heart

> To vice's allurements not prone
>   Acknowledged the maid that was dear:—
> Ready Hymen soon fastened the tie:—
>   Ever blest be the date of that year!
>
> Many summers rolled on, full of joy,
>   Many winters that never were drear;
> And oft-times a girl or a boy
>   Gave delight to the date of the year.
>
> Bred in harmony, virtue and truth,
>   Happy faces around me appear;
> And the grateful affections of youth
>   Prove a balm to the date of the year.

The happy, grateful faces that appeared around Francis Newbery and enabled him to bask in the warm glow of

---

[1] Article in *Dictionary of National Biography*, contributed by Welsh.

self-approval were in fact evidence of the establishment of a dynasty. Francis's eldest son, John, educated at Eton and St John's College, Cambridge, became a colonel in the Army, but took over the business when his father died in 1818, and ran it in conjunction with his younger brother William for 36 years. The task appears not to have been onerous, for, according to his son Arthur, John "spent more time at the Senior United Services Club, Pall Mall, in the congenial company of his brother officers, than in St Paul's Churchyard at the business house."[1] In the next generation, Arthur and Lionel Newbery were in charge, and they were followed by their respective sons, Percy and Francis.

The firm, now a limited company, continued into the twentieth century. Dr James's Powder (*pulv. Jacobi vera*) was still being produced, and when the question of Goldsmith's death was revived in the London *Times* in 1930, Mr Francis Newbery came stoutly to its defence.

Early in 1964, when I was researching for my study of children's literature *Written for Children*, I found that the name of Francis Newbery & Sons Ltd was still in the London telephone directory. A letter of inquiry brought a reply from the managing director of May, Roberts & Co. Ltd., wholesale and manufacturing chemists, who had succeeded to the business. He told me that Dr James's Powder

> was a very small chemist line manufactured by Messrs Francis Newbery & Sons Ltd before the [Second World] War, and when our premises were destroyed at Clerkenwell Road, all papers and the formula were destroyed with them. One of my colleagues, who was in the business at that time, said that it was then decided it would not be worth while continuing manufacture, and so it was discontinued in 1941.

The "most powerful discovery in the annals of medicine" had passed into history.

---

[1] A. Le B. Newbery, *The Newberys in Six Generations*, p. 51.

APPENDIX

The Newbery Medal

THE JOHN NEWBERY MEDAL is awarded annually by the American Library Association for the most distinguished contribution to American children's literature during the preceding year. All forms of writing — fiction, non-fiction, and poetry — may be considered, but the work must be original and the author must be a citizen or resident of the United States. The winner is chosen by a committee of the Children's Services Division of the A.L.A. A companion award, the Caldecott Medal, named for the nineteenth-century English illustrator Randolph Caldecott, is made each year to the artist of the most distinguished American picture book for children.

The Newbery award winners from 1922 to 1994 were:

1922 Hendrick Willem Van Loon
The Story of Mankind

1923 Hugh Lofting
The Voyages of Doctor Dolittle

1924 Charles Boardman Hawes
The Dark Frigate

1925 Charles J. Finger
Tales from Silver Lands

1926 Arthur Bowie Chrisman
Shen of the Sea

1927 Will James
Smoky, the Cowhorse

1928 Dham Gopal Mukerji
Gay-Neck, the Story of a Pigeon

1929 Eric P. Kelly
The Trumpeter of Krakow

1930 Rachel Field
      *Hitty, her First Hundred
      Years*

1931 Elizabeth Coatsworth
      *The Cat who Went to
      Heaven*

1932 Laura Adams Armer
      Waterless Mountain

1933 Elizabeth Foreman Lewis
      *Young Fu of the Upper
      Yangtse*

1934 Cornelia Meigs
      Invincible Louisa

1935 Monica Shannon
      Dobry

1936 Carol Ryrie Brink
      Caddie Woodlawn

1937 Ruth Sawyer
      Roller Skates

1938 Kate Seredy
      The White Stag

1939 Elizabeth Enright
      Thimble Summer

1940 James Daugherty
      Daniel Boone

1941 Armstrong Sperry
      Call it Courage

1942 Walter D. Edmonds
      The Matchlock Gun

1943 Elizabeth Janet Gray
      Adam of the Road

1944 Esther Forbes
      Johnny Tremain

1945 Robert Lawson
      Rabbit Hill

1946 Lois Lenski
      Strawberry Girl

1947 Carolyn Sherwin Bailey
      Miss Hickory

1948 William Pène du Bois
      The Twenty-one Balloons

1949 Marguerite Henry
      King of the Wind

1950 Marguerite De Angeli
      The Door in the Wall

1951 Elizabeth Yates
      Amos Fortune, Free Man

1952 Eleanor Estes
      Ginger Pye

1953 Ann Nolan Clark
      Secret of the Andes

1954 Joseph Krumgold
      . . . And Now Miguel

1955 Meindert DeJong
      The Wheel on the School

1956 Jean Lee Latham
      Carry on, Mr Bowditch

1957 Virginia Sorensen
      Miracles on Maple Hill

1958 Harold Keith
      Rifles for Watie

1959 Elizabeth George Speare
      *The Witch of Blackbird
      Pond*

1960 Joseph Krumgold
      Onion John

1961 Scott O'Dell
      Island of the Blue Dolphins

1962 Elizabeth George Speare
      The Bronze Bow

1963 Madeleine L'Engle
      A Wrinkle in Time

1964 Emily Neville
      It's Like This, Cat

1965 Maia Wojciechowska
      Shadow of a Bull

1966 Elizabeth Borton de
      Trevino
      I, Juan de Pareja

1967 Irene Hunt
      Up a Road Slowly

1968 Elaine Konigsburg
      *From the Mixed-up Files of
      Mrs Basil E. Frankweiler*

1969 Lloyd Alexander
      The High King

1970 William H. Armstrong
      Sounder

1971 Betsy Byars
      Summer of the Swans

1972 Robert C. O'Brien
      *Mrs Frisby and the Rats of
      NIMH*

1973 Jean Craighead George
      Julie of the Wolves

1974 Paula Fox
      The Slave Dancer

1975 Virginia Hamilton
      M.C.Higgins, the Great

1976 Susan Cooper
      The Grey King

1977 Mildred D. Taylor
      *Roll of Thunder, Hear my
      Cry*

1978 Katherine Paterson
      Bridge to Terabithia

1979 Ellen Raskin
      The Westing Game

1980 Joan W. Blos
      *A Gathering of Days: a New
      England Girl's Journal,
      1830-32*

1981 Katherine Paterson
      Jacob Have I Loved

1982 Nancy Willard
      *A Visit to William Blake's
      Inn: Poems for Innocent
      and Experienced Travelers*

1983 Cynthia Voigt
      Dicey's Song

1984 Beverly Cleary
      Dear Mr Henshaw

1985 Robin McKinley
      The Hero and the Crown

1986 Patricia MacLachlan
      Sarah, Plain and Tall

1987 Sid Fleischman
      The Whipping Boy

1988 Russell Freedman
      Lincoln: a Photobiography

1989 Paul Fleischman
      *Joyful Noise: Poems for
      Two Voices*

1990 Lois Lowry
      Number the Stars

1991 Jerry Spinelli
      Maniac Magee

1992 Phyllis Reynolds Naylor
      Shiloh

1993 Cynthia Rylant
      Missing May

1994 Lois Lowry
      The Giver

Details of winners from *The Newbery and Caldecott Awards: a Guide to the Medal and Honor Books*, published by the American Library Association

BIBLIOGRAPHY

Ashton, John	*Chapbooks of the eighteenth century*, London, 1882.
Ashton, John	*Social life in the reign of Queen Anne*, London, 1882
Berkshire (formerly *Reading) Mercury*	250th anniversary supplement, July 12, 1973.
Buck, J.D.C.	*John Newbery and literary merchandising, 1744-67*, doctoral thesis, University of California, Berkeley, 1972.
Burton, K.G.	*The early newspaper press in Berkshire (1723-1855)*, privately published, Reading, 1954.
Colman, George	*Terrae-filius*, No 3, reprinted in *Prose on several occasions*, London, 1787.
Darton, F.J. Harvey	*Children's Books in England*, 3rd edn, revised by Brian Alderson, Cambridge University Press, 1982.
Devlin, Christopher	*Poor Kit Smart*, Hart-Davis, London, 1961.
Dictionary of National Biography	Essays on Peter Annet, Oliver Goldsmith, John Harris, Francis Newbery, John Newbery, Ralph Newbery, Thomas Newbery, Christopher Smart.
Dobson, Austin	*Life of Oliver Goldsmith*, London, 1888.
Forster, John	*Life and adventures of Oliver Goldsmith*, London, 1848.
Foster, Sir William	*England's quest of eastern trade*, London, 1933.
Gibbs, J.M.W.	*Works of Oliver Goldsmith*, new edn, London, Bohn, 1884.
Ginger, John	*The notable man* (Goldsmith), Hamish Hamilton, London, 1977.
Gottlieb, Gerald	*Early children's books and their illustration*, Pierpoint Morgan Library with Oxford University Press, 1975.

Grey, Jill E.

The Lilliputian Magazine — a pioneering periodical? Article in *Journal of Librarianship*, Vol 2, No 2, April 1970, pp.107-115.

Hakluyt, Richard

Principall Nauigations, Voiages, & Discoveries of the English Nation, etc. etc., London, 1598-1600, and in several other editions.

Hunter, C.

Prefatory essay to *The Poems of the late Christopher Smart, M.A.,* Smart & Cowslade, Reading, and F. Power & Co., London, 1791.

Irving, Washington

Oliver Goldsmith: a biography, London, 1849.

Johnson, Samuel

The Idler, London, 1758-60.

Jones, Stephen

A new biographical dictionary, London, 1796.

Knight, Charles

Shadows of the old booksellers, London, 1865.

Locke, John

Educational writings, Cambridge University Press, 1922 (and other editions.)

Marble, Annie Russell

From prentice to patron: the life story of Isaiah Thomas, D. Appleton & Century, 1935.

Meigs, Cornelia and others

A critical history of children's literature, new edn, Macmillan, New York, 1969.

Newbery, Edmund

The Newberys, privately published, London, 1960.

Newbery, Francis

Donum Amicis, verses on various occasions, privately published, London, 1815.

Newbery, A. Le Blanc

The Newberys in six generations, privately published, High Barnet, 1911

Percy, Thomas

Introduction to *Works of Oliver Goldsmith,* London, 1801.

Prior, James

Life of Oliver Goldsmith, London, John Murray, 1837.

Roberts, R.J.

The 1765 edition of Little Goody Two-Shoes, *British Museum Quarterly,* No 29 (summer 1965), pp. 67-70.

Roscoe, Sydney

John Newbery and his successors, 1740-1814: a bibliography, Five Owls Press, Wormley, 1973.

Rosenbach, A.S.W.

Early American children's books: with bibliographical descriptions of books in his private collection, Southworth Press, Portland, Maine, 1933.

Shipton, Clifford J.

Isaiah Thomas: Printer, Patriot, and Philanthropist, Leo Hart, Rochester, N.Y., 1948.

Thwaite, M.F.	*From primer to pleasure in reading*, new edn, The Library Association, London, 1972.
Thwaite, M.F.	Introduction to facsimile of *A Little Pretty Pocket-Book*, Oxford University Press, 1966.
Townsend, John Rowe	*Written for children*, 5th edn, Bodley Head, London, 1990.
Tragen, Cecil	*Elizabethan Adventure*, Witherby, London, 1953.
Welsh, Charles	*A bookseller of the eighteenth century*, Griffith, Farran, Okeden & Welsh, London, 1885.
Welsh, Charles	Introduction to facsimile of *Little Goody Two-Shoes*, Griffith & Farran, London, 1881.

INDEX

ABOUT THE AUTHOR

JOHN ROWE TOWNSEND was born in Leeds, England, and took an honors degree in English at Cambridge University. He worked as a reporter on the *Yorkshire Post* and *Evening Standard* before joining the *Manchester Guardian* in 1949. After being a sub-editor and later Art Editor, he edited the paper's weekly international edition until 1969, when he left to become a professional writer. He retained a connection with the *Guardian* as children's books editor until 1978 and as a columnist until 1981.

He has published more than twenty books for children and young people, mostly with Oxford University Press or Penguin Books in Britain and with Lippincott (now part of HarperCollins) in the United States. He has also written three books for adults on children's literature and an adult novel, and has edited an Oxford poetry anthology. For several years he was an adjunct professor at the Simmons College Center for Children's Literature in Boston, Massachusetts, and he is currently an adjunct board member of Children's Literature New England. He has lectured on children's literature in Britain, the United States, Canada, Australia and Japan.

Honeſty
is the beſt Policy ;
Honeſty
and
Induſtry
perform Wonders.